PREACHING IN THE SUNDAY ASSEMBLY

Preaching in the Sunday Assembly

A Pastoral Commentary on *Fulfilled in Your Hearing*

COMMENTARY AND TEXT

The Catholic Association of Teachers of Homiletics

James A. Wallace, C.Ss.R., Editor

LITURGICAL PRESS
Collegeville, Minnesota

www.litpress.org

1	2	3	4	5	6	7	8

Library of Congress Cataloging-in-Publication Data

Preaching in the Sunday assembly : a pastoral commentary on Fulfilled in your hearing : commentary and text / The Catholic Association of Teachers of Homiletics ; James Wallace, editor.
     p.   cm.
  Includes bibliographical references.
  ISBN 978-0-8146-3346-5 — ISBN 978-0-8146-3936-8 (e-book)
  1. Preaching.   2. Sermons.   I. Wallace, James A., 1944–
II. Catholic Association of Teachers of Homiletics.   III. Catholic
Church. National Conference of Catholic Bishops. Bishops'
Committee on Priestly Life and Ministry. Fulfilled in your hearing.

BV4211.3.P733   2010
251.0088'282—dc22   2010020277

Contents

Editor's Preface

Although almost thirty years have passed since *FIYH* was first published, it remains a rich and respected guide for understanding, crafting, and engaging in the homiletic event. At the same time, there have been many developments and changes over these decades in such areas as cultural context, biblical interpretation, liturgical theology, and homiletic methodology that suggest the value of a critical revisiting of the document so that its initial forward trajectory can be maintained. This effort seems especially important because the United States bishops have signaled their intent to craft a new document that will either build upon or possibly supersede *FIYH* as the official statement of the United States church on preaching in the Sunday assembly. In light of these developments, this commentary will both commend the enduring strengths of *FIYH* and suggest where a new document could amend and even correct some of its elements.

All references to church documents will give paragraph numbers. Although the initial publication of *FIYH* did not provide paragraph numbers, for ease of reference this commentary will use the numbering found in Appendix A.

James A. Wallace, C.Ss.R.

Introduction

This pastoral commentary celebrates twenty-five years of *Fulfilled in Your Hearing: The Homily in the Sunday Assembly* (*FIYH*), published by the Bishops' Committee on Priestly Life and Ministry in 1982. In October 2008, the Synod on the Word of God in Rome marked another important moment in which the universal church stepped forward to reflect on the ministry of the Word in Catholic life. The very fact of this synod affirms the ongoing work of all who are committed to improving Catholic preaching.

The road that led to this pastoral commentary began with a close rereading of *FIYH* by the membership of the Catholic Association of Teachers of Homiletics (CATH) at an annual meeting in West Palm Beach in November 2006. CATH is a small but vital network for men and women who teach preaching in Catholic seminaries, schools of theology, deacon formation programs, and other ministry formation settings in the United States. In 2006, the United States Conference of Catholic Bishops invited CATH and several key Catholic organizations to give input about a possible new document on preaching. While thoughts of a new document were put aside until after the Synod on the Word of God, our CATH conversation triggered renewed appreciation of the profound influence that *FIYH* has made on preaching and preaching education these past twenty-five years.

Serendipitously, CATH was approached in 2007 with a generous offer to fund continued reflection on *FIYH*. This enabled a

CATH writing team to convene in St. Louis in September 2007 and April 2008. The funding also supported another annual meeting in St. Paul in November 2007 at which the entire CATH membership worked to conceive the scope and vision for this pastoral commentary on *FIYH*.

In these conversations, CATH welcomed two members of the original Priestly Life and Ministry subcommittee and writing team—William Skudlarek, O.S.B., the principal writer of *FIYH*, and Fred Baumer. Their stories about the subcommittee were so fascinating that CATH membership arranged for further interviews and research in order to include an appendix on the history of *FIYH* in this commentary.

The CATH writing team organized its work according to the original divisions found in the document: the assembly, the preacher, the homily, and homiletic method. The following is a listing of the members of the writing team and the sections on which they worked. When a section had a principal author, an asterisk (*) is placed after his or her name.

Project Direction
Fr. Gregory Heille, O.P., past-president of CATH and project director; Professor of Homiletics and Vice President and Academic Dean at Aquinas Institute of Theology, Saint Louis, Missouri; editor of *Theology of Preaching: Essays on Vision and Mission in the Pulpit* (Melisende, 2001)

Editor
Fr. James A. Wallace, C.Ss.R., editor of the commentary; Professor of Homiletics at Washington Theological Union, Washington, D.C.; author of *Preaching to the Hungers of the Heart: The Homily on the Feasts and within the Rites* (Liturgical Press, 2002) and *The Ministry of Lectors*, 2nd ed. (Liturgical Press, 2004)

The Assembly
Dr. Miguel Díaz, Professor of Theology, The College of Saint Benedict, Saint John's University, and Saint John's School of Theology·Seminary, Collegeville, Minnesota

Fr. Jan Michael Joncas, Associate Professor of Catholic Studies, University of St. Thomas, Saint Paul, Minnesota; author of *Preaching the Rites of Christian Initiation* (Liturgy Training Publications, 1994)

Dr. Deborah Organ*, President of CATH; Clinical Social Worker and Pastoral Minister at Holy Rosary Parish, Minneapolis, Minnesota

The Preacher
Fr. Donald Heet, O.S.F.S., Secretary/Treasurer of CATH; Associate Clinical Professor and Director of Doctor of Ministry Program, Catholic University of America, Washington, D.C.

Sr. Theresa Rickard, O.P., President and Executive Director of RENEW International, Plainfield, New Jersey

Fr. James A. Wallace, C.Ss.R. (See under Editor)

The Homily
Fr. Guerric DeBona, O.S.B., out-going President of CATH; Professor of Homiletics, Saint Meinrad Seminary and School of Theology, Saint Meinrad, Indiana; author of *Fulfilled in Our Hearing: History and Method of Christian Preaching* (Paulist Press, 2005)

Fr. Edward Foley, O.F.M.Cap.*, Duns Scotus Professor of Spirituality and ordinary Professor of Liturgy and Music at Catholic Theological Union, Chicago, Illinois; general editor of *Commentary on the General Instruction of the Roman Missal* (Liturgical Press, 2007) and author of *From Age to Age* (Liturgical Press, 2008)

Sr. Mary Margaret Pazdan, O.P., Professor of Biblical Studies at Aquinas Institute of Theology, Saint Louis, Missouri; Promoter of Preaching for the Sinsinawa Dominican Sisters, Wisconsin; author of *Becoming God's Beloved in the Company of Friends: A Spirituality of the Fourth Gospel* (Wipf and Stock, 2007)

Homiletic Method
Dr. Fred Baumer, Vice President for Organizational Effectiveness at BI Worldwide, Minneapolis, Minnesota; co-founder

with Patricia Hughes Baumer of Partners in Preaching, Eden Prairie, Minnesota; lecturer in preaching at Saint John's School of Theology·Seminary, Collegeville, Minnesota; member of the writing team for *Fulfilled in Your Hearing* (NCCB, 1982)

Sr. Mary Margaret Pazdan, O.P. (See under The Homily)

Fr. William Skudlarek, O.S.B., Secretary General of the Monastic Interreligious Dialogue, Rome; principal writer of *Fulfilled in Your Hearing* (NCCB, 1982)

Sr. Honora Werner, O.P., Councilor to the Prioress of Caldwell Dominican Sisters, Caldwell, New Jersey; Director of the Doctor of Ministry in Preaching at Aquinas Institute of Theology, Saint Louis, Missouri

Appendix: A History of **Fulfilled in Your Hearing**
Ms. Trish Sullivan Vanni, doctoral student at the Graduate Theological Union, Berkeley, California; Project Director of the Emerging Models of Pastoral Leadership Project

While the Bishops' Committee on Priestly Life and Ministry chose to address *FIYH* to priests and bishops presiding and preaching at the Sunday Eucharist, the introduction to *FIYH* acknowledges the role of deacons as ministers of the Word and also the responsibility of the entire Christian community, by virtue of baptism, for the proclamation of the Word of God. Clearly, *FIYH* has been read with great benefit by Catholic bishops, priests, deacons, and lay ecclesial ministers, all dedicated to the proclamation of the Word of God. On careful consideration of today's ministerial context, the Catholic Association of Teachers of Homiletics chose to address this commentary to all Catholics charged by virtue of their ministry with proclaiming the Word of God, as well as to seminarians, candidates for permanent diaconate, and other ministerial students taking their first courses in preaching. Keeping in mind the growing frequency in the United States of preaching in the absence of a priest, the writing team also chose to nuance such words in the original document as "Sunday" and "homily" with the use of additional expressions such as "the Lord's Day" and "the Word." We believe that both *FIYH* and this commentary can be studied with benefit by those who preside and preach at the Eucharist and by those who minister in the absence of a priest. Of course, we also welcome an international and ecumenical readership to *FIYH* and to this commentary.

Rather than taking a didactic approach to an inspiring document, we chose to proceed by way of commendation and recommendation. This allows for recognition of those insights and features of *FIYH* that continue to deserve notice and celebration. At the same time, attention can be given to present-day issues of cultural context and the wealth of emerging insights recently developed in the fields of biblical interpretation, liturgical theology, and homiletic methodology. The five areas of context, hermeneutics, liturgy, mission, and theology emerged in our discussions as helpful signposts or rubrics for organizing an examination of each section of *FIYH* with a view to making recommendations. We hope these recommendations will prove helpful to preachers and preaching students, as well as to bishops and their advisors, as we work together to address issues pertinent to preaching in today's church in North America. CATH hopes to be a vital partner in this continuing conversation.

Gregory Heille, O.P.

I: The Assembly

Deborah Organ (principal author),
Miguel Díaz, and Jan Michael Joncas

The 1982 document *Fulfilled in Your Hearing: The Homily in the Sunday Assembly* (hereafter, *FIYH*), began with a consideration of the gathered assembly as the primary context and starting point for preaching the Word. We affirm *FIYH*'s decision to make the assembly its starting point, and, in the first part of this section, we hope to provide additional nuance to its description of the assembly. Furthermore, we explore some practical implications for preaching that flow from the even more diverse contexts and characteristics of today's assemblies. In the second part of this section, we consider the impact of current ecclesial reality on the life and practice of local assemblies, as well as reflect on a methodology for developing the parish as a place where differences and even conflicts can be engaged in a way that creates a setting for liturgy, learning, and new life.

Diversity in Today's Assemblies: Characteristics and Worldviews

FIYH affirmed the importance of the preacher's knowing the assembly gathered for worship and made a creditable effort to identify ways in which assemblies may be diverse, recognizing this possibility even in congregations apparently homogenous.

Its analysis of diversity employed categories such as age, ethnicity, race, gender, and social and economic status (8). It also acknowledged the presence within the assembly of "the joyful and the bereaved, the fervent and the halfhearted, the strong and the weak" (8). These categories remain vital in our own day.

Consider a parish like San Jacinto. San Jacinto is a community of approximately nine hundred families centrally located in a large metropolitan area. Originally established sixty years ago to serve a Polish community, the parish continues to offer Mass in Polish occasionally, and the regular English Sunday liturgy is attended by a few elderly Polish speakers, along with approximately seventy English-speaking parishioners. The pews are jammed, however, at the later Spanish Mass with hundreds of mostly first-generation Mexican and Ecuadorian families. While a remnant of the English-speaking community still remains in charge of many of the parish's operations, newer Spanish-speaking parishioners are beginning to come forward in an effort to involve themselves in parish ministries and to express their formational and sacramental needs. Diversity is certainly present, as is the possibility for conflict, emerging around the use of parish meeting rooms and other resources. The parish is clearly at a crossroads in its identity and mission. The pastor wonders how to preach to his diverse community, both at the separate liturgies conducted for each language group and at the occasional bilingual liturgies the parish has recently, and somewhat tentatively, decided to try. Fortunately, there are resources available to help preachers like this pastor.

Culture as Dynamic and Transformative

Since the publication of *FIYH*, new resources have emerged that offer a framework for responding pastorally and homiletically to the culturally diverse characteristics and backgrounds found in parishes like San Jacinto. In *Preaching to Every Pew: Cross-Cultural Strategies*, James R. Nieman and Thomas G. Rogers identify culture as a broadly inclusive category of diversity in that many of the ways that people differ involve some aspect of their cultural worldview (Nieman and Rogers, 15). The authors stress the dynamism of culture, noting that, while there may be essential dimensions of culture that remain constant throughout our lives, we are also engaged in a continual process of exploration, transformation, and learning in relation to our culture of origin and its influence on us and, even more so, when we have moved into a different cultural context. For example, immigrants who have lived awhile in the United States frequently go back to their countries of origin to visit and discover how much they themselves have changed. While they may have continued to live into and out of their original cultural heritage, they also have been engaged and influenced by the cultural forces of their new homeland. Some understanding on the preacher's part of the dynamics of cultural transformation is essential for preaching that connects with multicultural communities.

New expressions of faith are coming to birth in parishes that include significant representation by more than one cultural group. Often clergy who come to the United States from around the world to serve people from their own country of origin are surprised by how liturgy and faith expression have evolved from what they knew in their countries of origin. This is true even in parishes sensitive to providing an environment that affirms and attempts to preserve diverse cultural expressions of faith. There is movement in some United States parishes toward the creation of "intercultural community." This name was devised by Alejandro Aguilera Titus of the Secretariat for Hispanic Ministry at the United States Conference of Catholic Bishops to describe a parish community that seeks to maintain important cultural traditions by engaging in authentic and enriching dialogue with people of different cultural backgrounds, with the goal of becoming one community. This concept has been adopted as a central part of pastoral planning in Hispanic ministry by some local churches, including the Archdiocese of Minneapolis–St. Paul. Intercultural parish communities represent a significant move away from what can be called "parallel communities" that have been so common in United States Catholic dioceses for the last twenty-five to thirty years. In these parishes, two or three cultural groups use the same parish facilities but with complete autonomy. All too often one group experiences some degree of marginalization. The goal of the intercultural community is to have a true community of all groups while not losing diversity.

Bilingual or even trilingual liturgies are becoming more common in parishes, particularly on special occasions. Shared planning and a good deal of expertise are necessary in preparing for these events, so that these occasions can provide the opportunity for everyone present to pray and participate. There is no getting around the fact that everyone sacrifices for bilingual liturgies, even the best planned ones, but there is the possibility that everyone will also benefit. Most people have a preferred language of prayer, and it is a sacrifice to have some elements of the liturgy in another language. The sacrifice is worth it, however, when people from the different language groups have begun to care about one another. If a parish has worked to bring people together in various contexts and valued relationships are forming, community members often become more motivated to pray together in the liturgy. The preaching, then, at bilingual and trilingual liturgies has the potential to build bridges, share differences, and foster unity.

Cultural Transformations, Negative and Positive

Cultural encounters and the resulting transformation can have a negative impact. A recent workshop in the highlands of Chiapas, Mexico, included role-playing by indigenous women exploring what they saw as the greatest challenges facing their communities. The first challenge they identified was dealing with the effects of migration. Their role-playing depicted a son returning to his family after a number of years in the United States; he had many new material possessions, but clearly had moved away from the collaborative mindset that is a core value of these indigenous communities. The women also reflected on the role that dominant cultural values in the United States, experienced either through migration or exposure to media, have played in the erosion of the moral fabric of their community through the introduction of permissive sexual mores.

Nevertheless, cultural transformation is often positive. The experience of "Aasha" is a case in point. She came from Somalia to the United States with her husband five years ago. They had one son when they arrived; then, a daughter was born in the United States. From the beginning of their ten-year marriage, Aasha's husband had beaten her regularly and, increasingly, severely. During a recent incident, a neighbor called the police and Aasha's husband was taken into custody, and she and the children spent a month in a domestic violence shelter. Through participation in a domestic violence survivors' group, Aasha's cultural belief that a husband had the God-given right to mistreat his spouse and children was challenged, and she developed new confidence in her own worth and in her ability to provide for her son and daughter. Without this exposure to another culture's relational values, no change is likely to have occurred.

The Fear Factor

An ecclesial community can be a place where people of different cultural backgrounds engage one another with mutual benefit. Such engagement must be intentional, since the potential always exists for the parish to increase the polarity between people with different characteristics, affirming stereotypes and increasing experiences of marginalization for at least one of the groups. Some long-time parishioners, for example, may resent people of different backgrounds who come to their parish speaking different languages. At the root of the resentment is often the fear of difference, as well as fear of losing the parish community they have known and loved. The homily can be one of the instruments for naming and confronting such fears while offering an alternative vision of what it means to be a Christian community, a pilgrim people, the body of Christ, empowered by the Holy Spirit to honor the gift of diversity and work toward ever greater unity.

Frameworks and Strategies for Preachers

Current resources have also reflected on what needs to be done to create liturgical environments where diverse congregations can pray and celebrate together. They agree on the importance of reflecting on the many nuances of diversity present in today's assemblies, so that fear of difference may give way to new understanding and respect. Nieman and Rogers suggest that preachers use four "frames" to identify common areas of diversity: ethnicity, class, displacement, and beliefs (Nieman and Rogers, 20). Their work includes naming the characteristics of each frame and offering some communication strategies useful for preaching. Cathy Black, in *Culturally Conscious Worship*, also names various elements for viewing diversity of background within an assembly, each in the form of a continuum, with a view toward balancing and blending elements in multicultural worship so that all can participate. For instance, she points out that some people experience God in a largely personal way, while others see God revealed more in community; some are well versed in doctrine, while others have little or no catechetical background. Black's work offers resources to assist preachers trying to respond to the challenge of congregational diversity in its many forms by broadening the repertoire of possible approaches and thereby leading to more effective preaching as well as the creation of "spaces" for dialogue.

As *FIYH* asserted, diversity encompasses categories other than race, culture, and ethnicity. These include age, gender, class, economic situation, and educational background. Andrew Carl Wisdom, O.P., in his book *Preaching to a Multigenerational Assembly* offers practical help to preachers wishing to address the generational diversity in their congregations. While people do not always fit neatly into any one generational group, such as the "Boomers" or "Generation X" in their faith expression, and while particular designations and descriptions will yield to others as a generation passes on, nonetheless, incorporating within a homily what Wisdom calls "generation specific cues," that is, illustrations and expressions designed to appeal to each age cohort, helps to assure that the message of a preaching event will both engage and be understood by all present. Such cues lead to and flow from what homiletician Joseph Webb calls "hub symbols" (Webb, 49). Wisdom proposes that Catholic preachers must understand the basic hub or core symbols of each generation, and go on to discover how the sacramental context of our liturgy offers transgenerational hub symbols (Wisdom, 59ff). From these the preacher can design a homily that is intergenerational.

Preaching has the potential to be either a barrier or a bridge to intercultural understanding. The relationship between the preacher and the assembly is a key component in developing homilies that foster and support a community's engagement with diversity, both within and outside the Christian community. Because many react to diversity with fear, dread, or weariness, it is crucial that preachers come to know their own people, so that homilies reflect and speak to the realities of human existence in this particular time and place, rather than speaking in generalities or reinforcing stereotypes of differing cultural characteristics. Preachers, as well as communities, may need to have their assumptions and judgments challenged. This is most likely to happen in ongoing relationships that go beyond the Sunday assembly, but it can begin with what is done in preaching.

By beginning with a call to focus on the assembly in its diversity, *FIYH* made a significant contribution to ensuring the relevance of the homily for its listeners. Over the last twenty-five years, the conversation this has provoked has grown and developed in significant ways, benefitting from the experiences of local communities like San Jacinto and through the work of theorists like Black, Nieman, Rogers, and Wisdom. Further assistance can be found in a more recent sociological study of American Catholics in *American Catholics Today* by William D'Antonio, James Davidson, Dean Hoge, and Mary Gautier.

Engagement of the Senses

Another contribution of *FIYH* is its call for preachers to engage the various senses in the preaching event. Such engagement is nothing new in Catholic life. Earlier generations may fondly recall the liturgical experiences of their youth that made use of incense, floral decoration, color, music, and other sounds to evoke a sense of God's presence and to call them to reverence. These have been as significant as the words of the liturgy in creating an effective setting for encountering the sacred. Throughout the history of the church in the United States, immigrants have brought their images and stories of how God has been present in the lives of their communities of origin, how Jesus has held the central place in the hearts and devotional life of the people, and how the Holy Spirit has taken a unique role in preserving their faith and trust in God. It is also common in many parishes in the United States to see shrines dedicated to Mary, Mother of Jesus, honored in various cultural expressions, a testimony to her instrumental role in the deepening of the community's faith in Jesus Christ.

Preachers do well to avail themselves of appeals to all the senses in preparing to preach. As oral and aural communication, preaching can engage the senses on multiple levels. Involving the imagination through sounds and images that evoke new perspectives on reality and new possibilities, rather than only describe them, goes far toward engaging a listener beyond the intellect alone. More resources for the development of imaginative preaching are available now than in 1982.

Engagement through Technology

Recent technological innovations in worship and preaching have met with mixed reviews. Some congregations have added screens to their sanctuaries, putting music and visual images up during liturgy. Sometimes projected images help to focus prayer; at other times they distract. Various efforts to respond creatively to the technological boom of the last decade have been made. One preacher even set up computer capability to text with teenagers in the congregation during his Sunday sermons!

While we believe it is important to acknowledge attempts to use technology to deepen community ties and improve the quality of the liturgical experience, it is equally important to critically evaluate them. In some cases, parishes may fall into the trap of replacing direct person-to-person communication with technology to the detriment of community growth. The use of technology in worship needs to be carefully monitored to assure it is enriching a community's faith formation rather than riding a current trend of offering entertainment.

Diversity in Today's Assemblies: Larger Ecclesial Currents and Contexts

While affirming the ongoing contribution of *FIYH* in calling preachers to recognize the diversity that exists within a community, we believe that the complexity of local assemblies deserves even further consideration. Such reflection necessitates taking into account insights gained from the perspective of several larger influences on a community's identity and liturgical life. We do not claim to include here all of the larger trends that affect parish life, such as the impact of present-day political and global issues, nor will we speak directly to current social issues that threaten to tear parish communities apart. We do judge, however, that the polarity and conflict that are part of life due to systemic impact may be served by strategies we present in this section on the assembly. We now focus on systemic identity and mission within the larger Roman Catholic Church.

An Ecclesial—and Homiletic—Identity Crisis

Because contemporary assemblies include so many people of diverse cultural backgrounds and other differing characteristics, we no longer can assume a common faith experience uniting the participants in a Sunday assembly. Complicating matters further is the presence in the assembly of varying beliefs that are prioritized differently. This can have implications for what people expect from a homily. Some might desire to hear more on doctrinal and moral matters. In reaction to an age hesitant to affirm one truth over another, or any absolute truth at all, some may want their preacher to provide greater clarity and firm guidelines based on church teaching. Others may ask preachers to connect the Scriptures with their lives while allowing them room to arrive at their own applications to specific areas in life.

While everyone from the recent 2008 Synod of Bishops on the Word of God to Pope Benedict XVI to local bishops' conferences throughout the world to people in the pews on Sundays (and, in some cases, people who are no longer in those pews because of what they characterize as "bad preaching") is calling for better preaching, the universal church has yet to agree on what constitutes "good" preaching. Studying all official church documents over the last forty years reveals that both a scriptural/dialogical approach (as in *FIYH*) and a doctrinal/educational approach to liturgical preaching (as in John Paul II's *On Catechesis in Our Time* [48]) have found their supporters. Such diversity can, however, lead to an identity crisis for preaching. Here is one instance of how that tension was experienced

A Parish Battleground

Nearly eighty years ago, St. Barnabas Parish began as the hub of an urban neighborhood. Established by Irish immigrants, it remains largely Caucasian while including a number of African American and a few Asian families. For about the last twenty years the parish has been a microcosm of larger church identity, with a number of people who closely identify with the call of Vatican II for greater lay participation in the church and society, as well as a number of people who embrace the current movement to affirm and retrieve traditional devotional practices and greater understanding of the doctrinal content of the faith.

Over those years the parish has been served by two pastors. The first, a self-described liberal, preached regularly on the Second Vatican Council's call to be a community engaged in the pursuit of social justice. During his years at the parish, the more traditional Catholics felt significantly alienated, while those of like mind with the pastor established a number of social justice initiatives. The second pastor evidenced an interest and concern with doctrine. Those with a similar perspective were relieved at his arrival and felt that they could "come out of the shadows." The former group of parishioners, however, now felt alienated and displaced, although some were also pleased to see a resurgence in the participation of young people who seemed thirsty for knowledge about the church. Preaching in this community became a battleground between passionate people with different perspectives, though it must be acknowledged that still others did not care about these theological differences but came to church for different reasons.

Preaching in a Polarized Context

One danger of preaching in a polarized context is that the preacher's perspective will contribute to making whole groups of people invisible. The story of St. Barnabas signals the importance of the preacher's self-knowledge and willingness to move beyond one's subjective perspective in order to relate to the parish community. When an assembly includes people with different perspectives on current ecclesial "hot-button" issues, whether social or sexual, political or theological, differences frequently are glossed over or the parish becomes a battleground. The reality and challenge of real differences in parish communities make it necessary to go beyond the relationship between preacher and congregation as emphasized in *FIYH* to the development of relationships between members of the community themselves. In order to offer a foundation for this assessment, we appeal to some theological roots of the Catholic tradition.

Diversity and the Trinity

While the above reflections on diversity and context may appear to be largely sociological and anthropological, we believe that the relationship between diversity and unity merits specific attention here and, in fact, is at the heart of our Catholic faith and doctrine. We wish to underscore ~~diversity as a positive~~ reality to be lived with and engaged, rather than a negative challenge to be reduced and overcome. *FIYH* tends to treat diversity as a problem to be "solved" by appeal to a common faith. The document argues: "While the diversity of every assembly is a factor that needs to be taken seriously by the preacher, and all the more so when the diversity cuts across racial, ethnic, economic, and social lines, this diversity should not blind us to another even greater reality: the unity of the congregation" (9). In such a view, diversity seems more a hurdle to be cleared than a gift to be cherished.

FIYH does not sufficiently articulate that the unity achieved through faith in Christ can only be brought about *in* and *through* diversity. We must keep in mind how the doctrine of the Trinity offers an invaluable resource for understanding how plurality is not an obstacle but is essential in constituting and safeguarding the unity of faith. Our communion with each other is grounded in a shared faith in God who reaches out to us "finally sending his only Son in human flesh." This Son Jesus, who "expressed the fullness of the Father's love by accepting death on the cross," is now glorified by the Father, and we, as believers, now witness to the kingdom of God "present both in and through Jesus, and still to come to its fullness through the power of the Holy Spirit" (10). Simply stated, the Trinitarian relationships in the one God frame the way in which we know God and the way in which we are called into the new community of the kingdom together.

Out of this Trinitarian perspective we focus on developing communities of dialogue and moving away from polarity. In practical terms, we experience unity in Christ through relationship in community, in all of its grace and messiness. How is it that diverse, often polarized, assemblies can create the context for living out of this diversity-in-unity in the here and now? While good preaching is only one factor in a community's engagement with both conflict and diversity, it is certainly an important one. Sunday homilies can lift up, name, challenge, and affirm the work that the community does all week long to bring faith and life together and extend that engagement to other settings in which its members find themselves. Preaching can help create the context where some very difficult but necessary conversations can begin.

Creating a Context for Dialogue in Assemblies

In 1999, the Harvard Negotiation Project published *Difficult Conversations: How to Discuss What Matters Most* by Douglas Stone, Bruce Patton, and Sheila Heen. Its first premise was that many interactions, particularly if they involve conflict, are "battles of messages" in which each participant is attempting to prove that he or she is right. The result of these "battles" is seldom dialogue, but rather power struggles. It is possible, however, to transform difficult conversations into learning ones that allow participants to maintain their perspectives while actually learning something about people who may view things differently. If we go into a conversation needing to win, then whoever is on the "other side" or has a different perspective cannot be right, because then we would be wrong—and lose!

Polarity in parish communities deepens when conflict is seen as win-lose. Polarity also tends to deepen if conflict is not engaged at all but is brushed under the rug on the mistaken assumption that people of faith will naturally do their best to "get along" and live without conflict. But when passionate people come together, difficult conversations *will* occur due to the high level of importance placed on matters of faith not agreed on.

Difficult Conversations reframes conflict and difference from win-lose situations to learning opportunities. The strategies provided may be useful for parishes looking to form a setting for dialogue. Such interaction can be nurtured by preaching that opens the door to a positive and enriching engagement of diversity. For example, if a parish forum is organized so that parishioners can air their perspectives on an important church issue, laying ground rules that reinforce listening to learn rather than to win, this effort may significantly and positively impact the experience for parishioners without denying differences and conflict.

Homiletic preaching can pick up the threads of the conversations happening within and even outside of the community. Preachers, while speaking with integrity from their own perspective, can deepen the dialogue within a community and reinforce the work being done. Such reflection makes it necessary for the preacher to be part of the ongoing dialogue and foster an environment of openness and safety for people of diverse backgrounds and perspectives. If the preacher has a significant leadership role in the community, whether and how that person engages dialogue and conflict may also impact the hearing of the Sunday preaching by some of the faithful. The need for continued development of seminary and lay ministry formation in both homiletics and conflict management is clear.

Clergy Demographics and Community Blending

It would be irresponsible to write a piece on the Sunday assembly in the twenty-first century without referring to the continuing shift in Catholic clergy demographics. Both the continued decline in the number of priests and the growth of lay ecclesial ministry have influenced the composition of assemblies in significant ways. Dioceses all over the country are restructuring their parishes, resulting in the blending of parishes with very different histories. Talk about difficult conversations! The process of renaming the new parish resulting from the merging of three small rural parishes in the Upper Midwest is fraught with as many potential cultural pitfalls as is the most urban multicultural parish. Diocesan planning is also presenting new configurations of professional parish leadership, and, in some places, those leaders are trained laypeople. The implications for the ministry of preaching are many and, as yet, largely unexplored.

The priest serving as pastor to three or more parishes is one result of shifting ecclesial demographics. This phenomenon has recently been explored in depth and breadth by Katarina Schuth, O.S.F., in her book *Priestly Ministry in Multiple Parishes*. Schuth gathered data from approximately one thousand priests for the book. The results of her survey that provide information on their quality of life were largely uplifting—most of the priests (over 97 percent), having to devise new ways to connect with their various congregations, reported high or moderate satisfaction with their relationships with parishioners (see *Priestly Ministry*, appendix B, question 49). The study confirms the enduring value and importance of relationship as the basis of parish life, and thus of effective preaching, and indicates the need to continue to develop models of preaching that meet the needs of new and different configurations of parish communities.

Conclusion

In many respects, the San Jacinto and St. Barnabas parishes are dealing with the same issue: how to engage diversity to further the growth and life of a unified assembly, rather than to bring about stagnation and polarization. Both examples point out that diversity has many faces in today's assemblies, and they affirm that the church continues to be transformed both by its leaders and people and what they bring to the assembly, as well as by larger trends taking place in society. Preaching, as a form of communication at the heart of parish life, can play a decisive role in forming the identity of the assembly, leading it toward either communion or polarization. That is a choice preachers and communities make every Sunday and throughout the week.

We affirm the vision of *FIYH* for homiletic preaching as beginning with the assembly in its diversity and unity, recognizing that the ecclesial environment has changed since 1982 and that the identity and composition of local assemblies continue to shift and change. We are grateful for the resources developed during these years that offer frameworks and practical helps for preachers and assemblies. This work enables preachers to carry on the dialogue essential to the development of preaching that is truly "a scriptural interpretation of human existence which enables a community to recognize God's active presence, to respond to that presence in faith through liturgical word and gesture, and beyond the liturgical assembly, through a life lived in conformity with the Gospel" (81).

II. The Preacher

Donald Heet, O.S.F.S., Theresa Rickard, O.P.,
and James A. Wallace, C.Ss.R.

The first reflection explicitly on the preacher in *Fulfilled in Your Hearing* occurs at the close of section 1 on the assembly (12–15), serving as a prelude to section 2 (16–39) and its extended treatment of the preacher. In these opening remarks, the preacher is identified as "a mediator of meaning," one who stands in the midst of the liturgical assembly "representing both the community and the Lord" (12), occupying a place in the "between," in the middle, between the God revealed in Christ and the community gathered in Christ's name, between the word of God spoken in the past and the word of God being spoken now in the world, especially in the lives of the assembly. By "making connections between the real lives of people who believe in Jesus but are not always sure what difference faith makes in life and the God who calls us to deeper communion with himself [*sic*] and with one another" (15), preachers fulfill their office of offering a word of meaning to their listeners.

Section 2, then, develops how this task of mediating meaning is to be carried out, calling for preachers to become attentive listeners to the many ways God continues to "speak," namely, through the Word of God in the Scriptures, and then through the Word of God in the lives of the people (10), giving particular attention to the assembly being addressed—their struggles, doubts, questions, concerns, and joys. For this careful listening to happen, preachers must make prayer an integral part of homily preparation (22–24), engage in the study and exegesis of the Scriptures (25–30), and develop a facility for entering into conversation with contemporary culture and world and local events (31–35). Finally, preachers are called to recognize their human limitations and are reminded that what people want most from them is to hear not someone with all the answers but "a person of faith speaking to people about faith and life" (39).

The following comments aim to affirm the ongoing value of certain insights about the preacher found in *FIYH* and also to suggest areas needing further reflection in light of what has occurred since *FIYH* was published. We believe these observations have ongoing relevance not only for ordained preachers but for any others who preach in the eucharistic assembly and during worship services in the absence of a priest. Our comments are organized under the headings found in the document, acknowledging under each heading prevalent concerns and emerging issues.

The Pastoral Role of the Preacher

FIYH's insistence that preachers prepare by being in conversation with both the Scriptures and the community remains a significant contribution to Catholic homiletics. Such activity is pastoral in the best sense, shepherding the community to the pastures of nourishment that can be found in the Word of God. The importance of grounding preaching in Scripture is sounded again and again throughout the text, carrying out the admonition given in the *Constitution on Divine Revelation* that "all the preaching . . . should be nourished and ruled by sacred scripture" (21).

An example of the *FIYH*'s practical wisdom is found in its call for preachers to be listeners and students of all that brings understanding of the various worlds in which we live, of all that contributes to understanding our humanity and reverencing our world. Preachers appropriately are encouraged to draw on the insights of science, philosophy, the social sciences, the arts—both classical and popular—and all other disciplines and forms of entertainment that help shape and mold us. Preachers must always work to deepen awareness of the complex social, political, and economic forces shaping us, thereby gaining for themselves "an informed understanding of the complex world we live in" (34).

Finally, a comprehensive vision of the goal of the homilist is articulated in *FIYH*'s call for the homily to recognize God's active presence in life and then to lead people to respond in faith "through liturgical word and gesture" and by "living a life in conformity with the gospel" (81). In the homily, then, preachers provide the assembly with motive both to "lift up your hearts" in the great act of thanks and praise and to "go in peace, to love and serve the Lord," moving out into the world as a pilgrim people. *FIYH*'s understanding of this dual purpose of preaching is very much in line with Pope Benedict XVI's understanding of the homily in *The Sacrament of Charity* (*Sacramentum Caritatis*) as that which "relates the proclamation of the word of God to the sacramental celebration and the life of the community, so that the word of God truly becomes the Church's vital nourishment and support" (Benedict XVI 2007, 46).

In recognizing the ongoing value of viewing the preacher through the lens *FIYH* offers, preachers can find material for reflection and self-examination of what they are trying to do when they preach. Even so, there is room for further development that goes beyond what was set down over twenty-five years ago.

Beyond Being the Sole Mediator of Meaning

While affirming the ongoing value of seeing the preacher as a "mediator of meaning," offering an interpretive word, grounded in God's word, we suggest further refinement. This designation could imply that the preacher alone is able to mediate meaning, suggesting the community is relegated to a passive role. In this case, the preacher can appear to be presented as an oracle for the believing community, laying claim to special insight into the meaning of their lives and how God is presently acting there and in the world. While one accepts the reality of God's ongoing revelation in Scripture, tradition, and the teaching of the magisterium, it would be highly presumptuous to include the insights of the preacher in this listing.

The ability of preachers to mediate meaning for a faith community is contingent not only on their being dedicated servants and listeners for how God is speaking through all the means already mentioned but also of giving equal attentiveness to listening to how others are also hearing God speak to them. A preacher can only offer—not impose—a word of meaning for the gathered assembly, ideally a message arrived at through collaboration with others, both colleagues in the preaching task and other members of the believing community, especially those participating in the preaching preparation process, as *FIYH* suggests (106–8).

Beyond Being a Scriptural Interpreter of Human Existence

When *FIYH* was written, the new lectionary with its "richer fare" of a wider selection of readings from the Bible had only been in use for little over a decade. The role of Scripture as germane to preaching was a relatively recent emphasis. For generations preachers had looked more to the catechism as preaching's basic resource. For this reason, *FIYH* defined the homily as offering "a *scriptural* interpretation of human existence." In recent years there has been a growing consensus to nuance further the homily as a scriptural interpretation of human existence.

Sometimes a particular biblical text itself may need to be questioned, even challenged, or—on occasion—the particular readings for a given Sunday may not provide an adequate lens for interpreting the lives of those present. Furthermore, there is the value of making greater use of the liturgical texts as an essential resource for homiletic preaching, that is, the prayers and hymns, along with actions of the liturgy. Finally, an interpretive word can result not only from a single text or prayer but from placing the various texts of the lectionary and sacramentary in dialogue with each other, with the liturgical season, and with the community. From the *interplay* of texts, biblical and liturgical, sacramental actions, events in the local church, the larger community, and other significant world contexts, a fuller interpretation of the assembly and its life in the world can be achieved.

Encouraging Other (Non-Ordained) Preachers

We wish to express the hope that, should there be any future document directed toward those preaching, recognition, appreciation, and encouragement also be given to the dedicated lay and religious ecclesial ministers who are engaged in this task. This situation can no longer be considered "temporary." The encouragement and support of ecclesiastical leadership, both bishops and clergy, along with further training, needs to be offered to those recognized as having the gift of preaching for the good of the community.

Listening and Praying

FIYH explicitly recognizes that preaching is more than simply "speaking about" Scripture; effective preaching takes its shape from the "dialogue between the Word of God in the Scripture and the Word of God in the lives of his people" (20). For this dialogue to occur, preachers must be listeners; indeed, listening must be "a way of life" (20). *FIYH* holds up listening to the Scriptures and to the people to whom one will preach as "a form of prayer, perhaps the form most appropriate to the spirituality of the priest and preacher" (21), calling on preachers to put prayer at the heart and center of their preparation for preaching by spending time each day in prayerful meditation on the upcoming Sunday readings and in a prayerful dwelling with their people, bringing their congregation to the Lord in prayer. This comprehensive view of spirituality is one of the jewels this document offers its readers.

A Preacher's Spirituality

While *FIYH* lays an excellent foundation for a spirituality of preaching with its emphasis on listening to the Scriptures, to the experiences of the people, and to the events occurring in the world, a preacher's spirituality is more than a listing of necessary activities for preaching well. Preaching the good news can serve as the integrating action that brings into harmony all the various pastoral activities in which preachers are involved, such as cele-bration of the sacraments, catechetics, administrative tasks, and all other ministerial work. As worthy and important as these other activities are, there is no pastoral activity that has the po-tential to touch as many people as effective liturgical preaching. To approach all other activities precisely as a preacher, as one listening for God's word, contributes to an integrated approach to ministry, since preachers who are committed to fostering dialogue in the act of preaching are also in a unique position to integrate that same dialogue in all areas of their ministry.

The Preacher and Lectio Divina (*Sacred Reading*)

Since *FIYH* stresses the importance of preachers listening to both sacred texts and the people of God, it may be helpful to offer some specific directions on how to do this. *FIYH* uses phrases like "prayerful listening," "praying over the texts," "daily meditation," and "dwelling with the texts of Scripture, knowing them and allowing themselves [preachers] to be known by them." A classical way of putting these prayerful activities into action is the ancient practice of *lectio divina,* or "sacred read-ing," a practice upheld in the final message of the 2008 Synod of Bishops on the Word of God (see *Origins*, Nov. 6, 2008: 345). While there are many different methods of interior prayer, *lectio* has the advantage of being specifically focused on the bibli-cal text. Its movement from reading to meditation to prayer to contemplation facilitates a deeper dialogue with Scripture, enabling "a prayerful reading in the Holy Spirit that is able to open to the faithful the treasure of the word of God and also to create the encounter with Christ, the living divine Word" (*Origins*, 345). Similarly, "listening" for the Word of God in the lives of the people involves more than being attentive and en-gaging in compassionate and active listening, as important as these are. The preacher also needs to be able to bring together in conversation the voices of Scriptures, the theological tradition of the church, and the experiences of the congregation. The skills of pastoral reflection are essential if the preacher is to minister to the community. As with prayer, there are a number of methods of pastoral reflection (see Krisak, *Handbook of Spirituality for Ministers*, 308–29).

Preachers have been given a great gift in their calling to the preaching ministry. Responsible preparation for preaching will, by its very nature, require them to engage in activity that will deepen their own spiritual life. As their ability to hear and preach God's word deepens, their relationship with God and God's people will grow as well.

Interpreting the Scriptures and Life

While the title of the third part in this section (25–36) is "Interpreting the Scriptures," its content also includes material that calls for the preacher to engage in interpreting the contemporary situation of the assembly. This section is to be commended for emphasizing the importance of interpreting both arenas. In 1982, it was groundbreaking to name the assembly as the starting point for understanding God's Word. By identifying both the assembly and the Scriptures as critical interpretive partners in the preaching conversation, *FIYH* invited the preacher to move from merely distilling information on the Scriptures, or on looking to the Scriptures only for doctrinal instruction, to delivering an event-filled Word, which found its goal in transforming a particular community of believers by enabling them to recognize the living God in their lives. In a future document on the homily, some of the more recent hermeneutical contextual methods of interpreting the scriptural and liturgical texts need to be taken into account. More will be said about this.

FIYH has had a significant impact on the formation of preachers in its call to acquire skills in biblical exegesis, theological exploration, and the study of the local and global context of the gathered assembly. In addition to encouraging preachers to be immersed in contemporary forms of culture, such as the arts and popular media, in order that they may address relevant issues in the local and global situation, preachers are also directed to attend to a homily's "form" (13). Form affects the way a preacher speaks. Preachers need to know and assimilate both the way their hearers talk and listen so that they communicate God's Word effectively. *FIYH* encourages preachers to speak the Word "in languages and images that are familiar to the dwellers of the particular avenue we are traveling" (14).

The Limitations of the Preacher

The concluding topic on the preacher offers a word of caution. Preachers can forget that this ministry has boundaries. Preachers have no claim to infallibility. They preach to advance the reign of God. If what they say does not accomplish that end, it ought not be said. Preachers can be afflicted with a certain hubris, thinking they always know more than their listeners or always know what their listeners need to hear. Few, if any, issues can be met with a "one size fits all" solution. The call to preach is more truly an invitation to humility, both before God who entrusts us with this mission of speaking the Word for the good of the people, and before the people whose hearts are restless until they rest in God. *FIYH* reminds preachers that they contribute best by "offering a Word which has spoken to their own lives and inviting the people to think and ponder on that Word so that it might speak to their lives as well. . . . What preachers may need to witness to more than anything else is the conviction that authentic mature faith demands the hard struggle of thinking and choosing" (38).

Proclaiming God's Justice

Other concerns present themselves at this time: environmental, social, economic, and ecclesial. While preachers cannot be experts in every field, and while certain fields can be looked upon as loaded with land mines that a preacher might prefer to avoid, still those called to preach are commissioned to speak a just word, calling the faithful to work for God's justice in the community and in the world, urging others to live in proper relationship to God, each other, and the earth that has been entrusted to our stewardship. Claiming personal inadequacy or avoiding necessary study of difficult matters is not a valid excuse for avoiding this task. Preaching marked by platitudes and generalities easily becomes irrelevant. Preachers should be willing to speak boldly about the demands of the reign of God.

Official church documents from the Vatican, the USCCB, and the local ordinary can be helpful resources when addressing controversial contemporary issues, grounding what is being preached in the church's authoritative teaching, not the preacher's own political or subjective preference. Similarly, the preacher is called to enable the congregation to look beyond the issues facing the local church and the local community to see the realities confronting and often threatening our brothers and sisters in other parts of the world.

Skill in Language and Cultural Competence

FIYH concludes its section on the preacher by holding up the desire of the people of God "to hear a person of faith speaking." Today, more than a quarter century later, we might specify that desire even more: the people of God want to hear a person of faith speaking in a language and in a way they can understand. Simply put, there is no pastoral benefit to people being subjected to a homily either given in a language the people do not know or delivered with an accent that makes comprehension difficult, if not impossible. Two situations come to mind. One concerns congregations with a significant number of worshipers who speak and understand only a language other than English—Spanish, Vietnamese, Tagalog, and Korean are a few possibilities. Clearly, such congregations need preachers who both speak their language and have a profound awareness of their people's culture. Several dioceses now require future preachers to be proficient in at least two languages. Such a policy has become even more necessary in the multicultural Catholic Church in the United States.

Furthermore, with the declining number of priests native to the United States, an increasing number of international priests are being recruited to minister here. The necessity of assisting these clergy brought in from other lands and cultures must be taken more seriously than it has been. Acknowledging the generosity of those willing to minister here and leave their own country, church leaders also need to consider the preaching competency of those coming to this culture. This includes, yet goes beyond, offering assistance in accent reduction. Providing the means for preachers to become acculturated to the community they have come to serve is equally necessary. Programs have been designed both to improve language skills and to assist in inculturating priests now ministering in a culture very different from their culture of origin. Bishops are urged to make these programs mandatory.

The ongoing legacy of *FIYH* includes an emphatic call to preachers to speak the language of faith that their people can understand. This call goes beyond the specific languages spoken in a particular community and beyond having a facility with the language of the various biblical, theological, and liturgical disciplines involved in competent preaching to include also the ability of a person of faith to communicate with the minds and hearts of one's listeners. The art of preaching involves speaking with clarity, coherence, and creativity. The language of the poet and the storyteller is crucial to the preacher, language that *FIYH* describes as "specific, graphic, and imaginative" (67).

Finally, pastoral concern also leads us to note the importance of increasing the number of those delegated to preach, especially when competent lay ecclesial ministers are available. Hearing the same voice, week after week, year after year, places an unnecessary limitation on God's word being heard in fresh and new ways and puts a great burden both on the preacher carrying this responsibility and on those listening. There was wisdom in Jesus sending the disciples out in twos.

III. The Homily

Edward Foley, O.F.M.Cap. (principal author),
Guerric DeBona, O.S.B.,
and Mary Margaret Pazdan, O.P.

The homily, like the liturgy that is its essential setting, is first and foremost an event. It is true that the homily often is transcribed in some written form and also that writing is a valuable stage in preaching preparation. Even so liturgical preaching is not a text, just as music is not notes on a page and liturgy is not a ritual book. At least theoretically, you cannot "write" a homily but only deliver one. Consequently it is helpful to think of both liturgy and its preaching more as verbs than nouns, events than ideas, encounters than commentaries. *Fulfilled in Your Hearing* has been very influential in helping preachers and communities to grasp more fully these dynamics of the homiletic act. It also makes an ongoing contribution in helping to initiate new preachers into a more holistic vision of the homily, resonant with the liturgical vision embedded in the *Constitution on the Sacred Liturgy* (*CSL*).

This revisiting of the ways in which *FIYH* defines and interprets the nature of liturgical preaching begins with a profound sense of admiration and gratitude for what was achieved in that pioneering document. For many preachers, even in the decades after *CSL*, the sermon was ordinarily the exposition of some dogmatic teaching or moralizing on personal and societal behaviors. *FIYH* was a potent antidote to such trends, effectively steering Roman Catholic preachers from sermonizing to liturgical preaching, from an arbitrary syllabus of topics and concerns to unwavering respect for the lectionary as foundational for the homiletic act.

This section of the commentary revisits liturgical preaching in general and the homily in particular as (1) a contextual act, (2) a hermeneutical act, (3) a liturgical act, (4) a theological act, and (5) a missiological act. *FIYH* gives particular attention to the homily in section 3 (nos. 40–77), and this longest single section of *FIYH* will be at the center of these considerations. That being said, given the integrity of that document, it is necessary to recognize that there are many other places in that text where insights, definitions, and observations on the homiletic act take place. Thus, these commendations and recommendations are offered in light of the whole sweep of *FIYH* and not confined to section 3.

The Homily as a Contextual Act

Understanding Context

Context is increasingly recognized by Roman Catholic and other theologians as an essential component in theological reflection and a source of theological insight and wisdom. Broader and more dynamic than the concept of "culture," theologian Stephen Bevans believes that context encompasses four elements: (1) the experiences of a person's or group's personal life, i.e., the experiences of success, failure, birth, death, and relationship that affect the way we experience God; (2) culture; (3) the particularities of one's social location shaped by factors such as gender, education, wealth, and access; and (4) local and global powers of social change symbolized, for example, by contemporary communications and commerce (Bevans, 4–5). In many respects *FIYH* is consistent and strong in attending to the broad dynamics of context when it speaks about the homily. Numerous times, for example, the document notes the importance of listening to and engaging people's experiences in preaching preparation (e.g., 4, 12, 18, 21, 68, and 74). The very definition of a homily posited in this document indicates that the homily is a particular kind of interpretation of "human existence" (81) and that the assembly itself is what *FIYH* considers one of the three major elements of the preaching act (3).

As for Bevans's second definitional component of context, *FIYH* does give some attention to the surrounding culture. While it is somewhat oddly placed under the heading "interpreting the scriptures," there is some emphasis on the need for preachers "to engage in a critical dialogue with contemporary culture" (31). There is mention of "the great artistic and literary achievements of a culture" (31), literature, painting, sculpture, and music (32). Even "modern entertainment media" such as television is mentioned, as is the theater (32). There is a somewhat less affirming recognition of popular forms of entertainment such as soap operas, baseball, and the latest hit albums (33), with a clear prejudice for the fine arts.

The third and fourth parts of Bevans's understanding of context get less attention in this document and seem less essential to both the shaping and delivery of the homily. There are some references to diversity in gender and age (8, 12), and a very strong admonition regarding the potential for exclusion of women (8), but such references do not seem to have a defining role in presenting the homiletic act. One cannot construct and deliver the same homily to a community mostly composed of women, and to an elderly congregation, and, again, to one composed mostly of young adults. *FIYH* implicitly acknowledges this (56), but gives little effective direction for shaping the homiletic event across educational and class distinctions. There is mention of racial and ethnic differences (9) and a general admittance of "the many forms of discrimination in our society" (74). Yet, given that the racial, ethnic, and cultural diversity of the United States is more marked today than any time in its history, making this country one of the most multicultural countries in the world, any successor to *FIYH* will need a more thoughtful and sustained reflection on what it means to preach in the midst of and across such diversity, which is often the basis of racism and discrimination.

FIYH is somewhat stronger in attending to global and political forces, noting that it is essential for preachers to understand the surrounding social, political, and economic forces (34). On the one hand, it also makes some allusions to communications—particularly in regard to entertainment (32), and it shows sensitivity to the influences of jobs, inflation, and wages (12). On the other hand, *FIYH* explores little of what difference these factors actually make or what authority they might possess in the homiletic event, observing only that the preacher need attend to them.

Enhancing the Role of Context

These reflections lead to three basic recommendations for how any successor to *FIYH* could enable preachers to homilize as a contextual event. First, the document is so singular about stressing that the homily is a scriptural interpretation—a topic to which we will return—that, to the extent that the context is acknowledged, it can appear more as an object of interpretation than its own hermeneutical lens in the preaching, more a set of examples (e.g., the arts) or a place where the hearers make a faith response to the homily than a powerful conversation partner in the homily itself (47). This is starkly demonstrated in two ways in the document. First, the context is not considered a major element in liturgical preaching (see below, part 3). While there is attention to the gathered community, the context is much larger than the gathered community, and sometimes the community needs to be challenged to engage realities of local, national, or global contexts—for example, racism. A second demonstration of the somewhat peripheral nature of context to the homily is the suggested model for homily preparation in a group (106–7), in which there is virtually no attention to contextual realities beyond the personal stories that one brings to the process (e.g., 108.4–5). Context matters and matters mightily. It must be one of the primary elements and dialogue partners in the homiletic event.

One minor recommendation on enhancing and respecting the role of context in the homily in any revised form of this document is a more expanded vision beyond the parish. The Catholic parish is certainly a very important place for the homily (6–8). But believers also experience liturgical preaching in nursing homes, military bases, college campuses, prisons, and retreat centers. *FIYH* seems to have almost a univocal vision of parochial preaching, and one that seems to tilt toward the middle class and U.S. dominant culture, e.g., in the aforementioned preference for fine arts over folk arts (32) and in the instinct to note people who have a "salary" (12) but not those who earn an hourly wage.

Finally, there does seem to be an optimistic, almost Rahnerian, view of the context here as more graced than flawed (e.g., 15, 45). While there is recognition of the struggles and pain in people's lives (e.g., 12, 74–75), there is yet continual reference throughout the document for the need to give "thanks and praise" (e.g., 14, 47, 48, 56, 68, 70, 71, 74–77, 108). For many people in the United States, however, the world is not a place of grace but of danger, and they are more easily drawn to lament than praise. Many of the psalms are laments (e.g., "Out of the depths I cry to you, O Lord"; Ps 130:1), and there is even an entire book of Lamentations in the Old Testament expressing Israelite suffering after the destruction of Jerusalem. Jesus himself calls out in lament on the cross (Mark 15:34). For those who suffer deeply from loss, abuse, discrimination, and suffering, lament is an important, even essential, move before one is capable of moving toward thanks and praise. While not suggesting that any such document should be pessimistic about the world, liturgical preaching needs to take into account not only the different life experiences of those in the assembly but also their different perspectives on the world. While we all share a common relationship with God through Christ in the Spirit, that is not to say that all members of a faith community "have a common way of interpreting the world around them" (10).

The Homily as a Hermeneutical Act

Broadly speaking, hermeneutics is the art of interpretation. While there are many hermeneutical theories operative for Roman Catholic preachers today, very often hermeneutics for preaching focuses on the interpretation of the scriptural texts that are proclaimed during the liturgy. The purpose of the hermeneutical enterprise is to offer a new understanding of a text, sometimes by questioning or even subverting the presuppositions that readers and hearers bring to a text, so that a powerful new meaning can be created.

FIYH clearly understands the homily as an interpretive act (e.g., 13, 44–46, 69, 81), and considers the preacher and, by extension, liturgical preaching as a mediator of meaning (e.g., 12–15). One way to explore how *FIYH* more particularly presents liturgical preaching as a hermeneutical act is to examine "what" is interpreted in and through the homily, "how" that interpretation takes place, "who" actually does the interpreting, and "why" that interpretation is constructed. In light of these four questions we will offer commendations and recommendations.

The "What" of Interpretation

As for "what" is interpreted, *FIYH* moves beyond the traditional thinking of its time, and consistently recognizes three elements that need to be interpreted in the homiletic act. First of all, it acknowledges that preaching is about offering people an interpretation of their lives in relationship to God (13). Indeed, the self-admitted understanding of the homily at the heart of this document is homily as an "interpretation of human existence" (81). Such an innovative perspective that places peoples' lives at the center of the interpretive act is a key contribution of this document well deserving of commendation. While given significantly less attention, *FIYH* also notes that the homily as a faith act is also concerned about interpreting the "world" (e.g., 44–46), or what we more broadly defined above as "context." This seems to confirm that the world or context should be one of the "major elements of liturgical preaching" (3).

Finally, *FIYH* is very strong on the homily as a *scriptural* interpretation of human existence that requires an interpretation of the assigned Scripture texts (e.g., 25–30). What is missing here is any attention to interpreting the *liturgy* itself, which, as we will discuss later on, is treated more as the immediate context for the preaching than actually one of the essential elements of the preaching. It is in the interplay and interpretation of the scriptural texts and the liturgical texts, actions, and objects, however, that we discover a lens through which to view human existence. This lens is not confined to the perspective provided by the Scriptures but arises out of the interaction between the biblical and liturgical components.

The "How" of Interpretation

As to "how" these three elements get interpreted, *FIYH* is strongest on its interpretive stance toward the Scriptures. The document is explicit about the need for exegesis (23–30), for reading the texts (86), particularly in the context of the Bible (87), and for ruminating and praying over and through the texts (20–24, 92). These are in service of a homily that does not so much explain the Scriptures as interpret people's lives through the Scriptures (52). One weakness here is that the approach to exegesis seems to favor historical-critical methods or what scholars sometimes refer to as the meaning "behind" the text (e.g., 53). Given the many advances in biblical hermeneutics over the past two decades, any successor to *FIYH* will have to address the contributions of the social scientific, literary, and other methods for exegesis. More will be said on methods of exegesis in the following chapter. The particular importance of story (cf. 66–67, 69) across cultures as an important way people interpret their own lives should suggest special attention to narrative methods as well. Finally, the lectionary is significantly different from the Bible and requires particular hermeneutical perspectives that *FIYH* does recognize, but in a quite underdeveloped way (87).

The "how" of interpreting peoples' lives and the world is admittedly more difficult (cf. 25 and 31) and less clear in *FIYH*. There is certainly a great deal of attention to listening to people's lives and praying over what has been heard (20–24). The image of "dwelling with . . . the people" is a powerful one (24). There is also the previously mentioned use of the arts as valuable interpretive lenses (31–33). There is a fleeting reference to social scientific methods (35) as possibly contributing to this interpretative task, but they are clearly optional here and are given no serious attention. Conversely, we would recommend that if the homily is to be a credible interpretation of people's lives and the broader context (e.g., "human existence," 81), then the liturgical preacher must have some rudimentary skills in social and contextual analysis so that these are credible voices in the theological reflection that gives birth to the homily.

The "Who" of Interpretation

The "who" of the interpretive act is somewhat weaker in *FIYH*, for two reasons. First, while admitting that there is a proposed homiletic method that does engage others beyond the preacher in shaping the homily (108), there is a very strong emphasis in this document on the preacher as the "mediator of meaning" (12). As has been noted in the last section on the preacher, *FIYH* presents a somewhat singular image of the preacher as the representative of the community who knows what congregations want and need to hear (4), articulates communal concerns, names the demons (13), and ultimately tries to make the connections between people's lives and God (5). The liturgical preacher is the listener and the prayer (20–24), who is called to dwell with the Scriptures and the people (24) in a singular way.

More problematic is the overall impression that the homily is a communicative act in which the interpretation, crafted by the homilist, is only received, heard, and accepted by an assembly that subsequently responds in faith (47–49). Contemporary philosophies and communications theories, however, recognize that the "listener" *is* also an interpreter, shares in the hermeneutical act, and actually constructs meaning rather than simply receives it. Since, as *FIYH* readily admits, liturgical preaching is an "encounter" (40) that should sound "like a personal conversation" (63), then it is essential to have a broader hermeneutical vision in which the assembly is one of the subjects and speakers in the conversation, with a distinctive responsibility for interpreting and constructing meaning in the homiletic event.

The "Why" of Interpretation

As for the "why" of this interpretive act, *FIYH* consistently speaks about the need for a faith response (e.g., 38, 47–49), which allows people to make connections between their lives and the

Gospel (19), to make sense of hardships in their lives (48), leading to deeper communion with God and one another (15). It is also clear that the homiletic interpretation is to lead to a more fruitful celebration of the Eucharist, which is the context for the homily (e.g., 11, 15, 43, 52, 60, 65). What seems to be missing here, however, are basic ethical foundations—such as love of neighbor, openness to the stranger, and the blessedness of peacemaking—that are essential validity tests for an authentic Christian hermeneutic. Interpretation by Christians does not ensure a Christian interpretation. Thus, it is essential that central Gospel values resound through the interpretive act of preaching. As previously noted, *FIYH* is fond of speaking about the need for giving "thanks and praise." The ancient liturgical motivation for giving such thanks and praise is that it is *justus* or "just." How does the hermeneutical vision embedded in *FIYH* honor God's preferential option for the poor at the heart of Roman Catholic social teaching? How does the call to love the stranger become definitional for what *FIYH* calls "Christian witness in the world" (43)? Here the insight of a hermeneut such as Sandra Schneiders might be valuable, as she calls for a "transformational hermeneutic praxis that will make the biblical texts available as a faith resource to the oppressed as well as the privileged" (Schneiders, *The Revelatory Text*, 1999, 5).

The Homily as a Liturgical Act

The *Constitution on the Sacred Liturgy* is foundational for clarifying that the homily not only takes place in the liturgy but is actually itself a liturgical act and "forms part of the liturgy" (52). *FIYH* embraces that insight, not only twice citing *CSL* on this point (42, 60), but further using the language of "integral" to explain the relationship of the homily to the liturgy (61). Compelling evidence that *FIYH* takes this integral relationship seriously are the multiple times the document underscores how the homily enhances the celebration of the Eucharist, noted above.

The strongest aspect of this liturgical vision of the homily comes through in *FIYH*'s continual emphasis on preaching the scriptural texts of the liturgy. This is one of the three major elements of the homily (2). *FIYH* believes the homily "flows" from these texts (42, 50, 61) and, as noted previously, the homily is defined, in part, as a "scriptural interpretation" (81). Consequently, *FIYH* provides one of the longest subsections of the document on "interpreting the Scriptures" (25–36); it regularly places Scripture in the first place in terms of what should be listened to or prayed (20, 21, 23, and 24); the first step in preaching preparation is to read the Scriptures (108); and, when outlining the non-negotiables of the homily, *FIYH* notes that the homily is to be "scripturally sound and pastorally relevant" (109).

The emphasis on preaching "from and through" the Scriptures (50) is commendable and, as previously noted, was a potent antidote to the trends of the day. The problem with this one-sided emphasis, however, is that *FIYH* suggests that apart from the readings, the rest of the liturgy is not a source for the liturgical preaching. In a statement memorable for capsulizing this one-sided approach, *FIYH* notes: "Just as a homily flows out of the Scriptures of the liturgy of the Word, so it should flow into the prayers and actions of the liturgy of the Eucharist which follows" (100).

In some respects this overemphasis on preaching the Scriptures is a result of the somewhat confused state of other church documents at the time. In the conciliar eagerness to embrace the Word of God and place it back at the center of church teaching and worship, *CSL* unfortunately described the Liturgy of the Word as the moment in which the readings are proclaimed and "explained in the homily" (24), an image repeated in the 1981 *Introduction to the Lectionary* (10). Echoes of this perspective are yet found in the 2002 *General Instruction of the Roman Missal* (*GIRM*) which speaks of the homily as "a living commentary on the word" (29) and employs the unfortunate phrase that the readings are "explained by the homily" (55).

A broader, more determinative vision is found in *CSL*'s central paragraph on the homily in which "the mysteries of the faith and the guiding principles of the Christian life are expounded from the sacred text during the course of the liturgical year" (52), a text repeated in the 1983 Code of Canon Law (c. 767, 1). The phrase "the sacred text" was clarified in the 1964 instruction *Inter Oecu-menici*, which commented: "A homily on the sacred text means an explanation, pertinent to the mystery celebrated and the special needs of the listeners, of some point in either the readings from sacred Scripture or in another text from the Ordinary or Prayer of the day's Mass" (54). *GIRM 2002* reflects this broader definition of the homily, which "should be an exposition of some aspect of the readings from sacred Scripture or of another text from the Ordinary or from the Proper of the Mass of the day and should take into account both the mystery being celebrated and the particular needs of the listeners" (65). Implicit here is the historical and doctrinal reality that it is the season, feast, or ritual event that sets the lectionary in the Roman Catholic tradition and not the other way around. The United States bishops actually go further in noting the appropriateness of preaching not only on the "sacred texts" but also on the liturgical rites and actions themselves (*Introduction to the Order of Mass*, 92).

Further homiletic reflection should emphasize that the homiletic act ordinarily engages the lectionary texts. At the same time, liturgical preaching cannot be limited to a "scriptural interpretation of human existence" (81) but needs to be expanded to a liturgical interpretation of human existence, of which the Scriptures are but one, albeit central, part. Doing so respects the tradition of the homily as a mystagogical reflection on the liturgy itself and asserts anew that it is the liturgy—not simply the Scriptures—that is dogmatically proclaimed as the source and summit of the church's life (*CSL*, 10). Such a liturgical lens is not an excuse to focus narrowly on the ritual actions and texts as though separated from the rest of our lives. Rather the centrifugal power of this liturgical lens must be unleashed, so that the liturgy of the church always leads us to faithful living in the "liturgy of the world" (Rahner, 169–70).

The Homily as a Theological Act

In many respects to speak of the homily as a contextual, hermeneutical, or liturgical event is already to make theological assertions about preaching. For example, to recognize that engaging the context is essential to the homiletic act is to admit theologically that God's self-revelation to humankind always occurs in the particularities of our existence. This theological stance is first of all rooted in the Judeo-Christian belief in creation as God's first revelation, and in the revelation that God intervenes in human history. Its particularly Christian roots are found in a theology of the central divine intervention we call Incarnation, and its corollary sacramental principle is that created matter and the work of human hands can be sources of revelation.

The goal of *FIYH* was not to set out a systematic theology of liturgical preaching. Rather, this document was addressed to clergy in pastoral ministry in the hopes of helping them become more effective preachers (*FIYH* introduction). Thus, while filled with many theological statements and presumptions, the document has no extended excursus on the theological foundations of the homily. It does, however, include many commendable insights that could be the starting point for a more developed theological perspective that, in turn, could also lead to more effective preaching. We highlight three of these here: the importance of the assembly, the significance of dialogue in general, and the broader emphasis on dialogue with the broader culture and the world.

Liturgical Action is Christ Acting, Head and Body

We have previously noted *FIYH*'s strength in acknowledging the importance of the assembly in the homiletic act. The explicit theological reason for doing so is contemporary ecclesiology, rooted in the *Dogmatic Constitution on the Church*, which recognizes Christ's presence in the church and in the assembly (5). While helpful, this perspective is somewhat underdeveloped, and any further homiletic development might do well to explore *CSL*, which provides important direction here, being quite explicit that every liturgical action is an action of Christ (7). It then goes on to clarify that an action of Christ is an action both of Christ, the head of the church, and his body, which is the church.

This insight provides an important corrective to any tendency to emphasize the preacher as the primary actor and interpreter in the homiletic act with the assembly being the receiver and respondent. While this might be true from some rhetorical perspectives, it is not true theologically. If every liturgical act is an action of Christ, head and members, and if, as *FIYH* asserts, preaching is itself a liturgical act (42 and 60–61), then from a theological perspective it is Christ head and members who are the primary actors and subjects of the preaching. Thus, from a theological perspective, the homily is less a point of "encounter between a local Christian community and its priest" (40) than it is an encounter between the local community and Christ, mediated by the homilist. Such a theological corrective even finds resonance in many contemporary communications theories (e.g., reader-response theories), which, as noted above, recognize that the "reader" or "hearer" is not a passive receptor of another's message but is an active interpreter and agent in the production of meaning.

Rooted in Trinitarian Theology and Communion Ecclesiology

A second useful insight about the homily from *FIYH* that could benefit from stronger theological foundations is the emphasis on dialogue, encounter, and conversation. While there is limited use of the term "dialogue" in the document (e.g., 20), there is much stress on listening (20–24) and responding (e.g., 11, 12, 45, 47–49, etc.). Furthermore, the emphasis on "conversation" as a model for the homiletic style seems to support a dialogical understanding of liturgical preaching. Theologically it might be helpful to ground this dialogic vision in a Trinitarian theology, which seems to be missing from this document. It is this aboriginal dialogue of love that is the Christian model for all discourse and community living. And it is this eternal discourse in charity that is both the model and source of all unity that *FIYH* believes is a central purpose of the homily (11). This Trinitarian emphasis could foreground more richly the role of the Holy Spirit, who not only has a role in the preparation of the homily (e.g., 21–22) but also animates all authentic Christian preaching (cf. 115).

Related to this Trinitarian recommendation is a further suggestion that any revisiting of *FIYH* consider the ecclesial foundations of the homiletic act in communion ecclesiologies. While

"communion" is a broad umbrella term that can designate sometimes strikingly different ecclesiologies, Dennis Doyle has suggested that it is possible to generalize about this ecclesiological
perspective as one that emphasizes relationships over juridi-
cal or institutional understandings of the church with a strong
emphasis on the mystical, sacramental, and historical (Doyle,
12–13). This ecclesiological perspective, which has been in as-
cendency since Vatican II, is resonant with a Trinitarian foundation of preaching and has particular affinities with preaching as
a liturgical act. Furthermore, it could provide a stronger theological foundation for negotiating the relationship between the
ministerial priesthood and the priesthood of the baptized with
which *FIYH* struggles (e.g., 17). In addition, it could provide a
more systematic way of thinking about how the homily at once
acknowledges diversity and at the same time strives for unity—
inviting people into a common relationship with God in Christ
through the Spirit while recognizing the myriad ways in which
such a relationship will be manifest in the body of Christ.

The Homily as a Missiological Act

Saying the homily must by definition be missiological is
grounded in the teaching of *CSL*, namely, that the liturgy, especially the Eucharist, is the source and summit of the church's life
(10). Mission is at the heart of the church's life, and, as the 1965
Decree on the Church's Missionary Activity (*DCMA*) reminds us,
the church is "missionary by her very nature" (2). Even more
striking is the teaching that it is from God's mission in the Son
through the Spirit that the church actually "draws her origin"
(2). Thus, one could conclude that the church is not so much a
church *with* a mission as it is a church *on* mission, and ultimately
exists *because* of God's mission.

Mission as Attentiveness to Spirit in the World

Mission in this broader sense is less about being sent to "con-
vert" another than about being attentive to how God's Spirit is
active in the world, sometimes in the most unlikely places and

among the most surprising people. The promise in this revelation is the possibility of "mission in reverse," in which preachers and other ministers "can and should learn from the people ministered to—including, and perhaps especially, from the poor and marginalized people" (Barbour, 304). The *DCMA* also acknowledges in its own way how the Eucharist is the source and summit of the church's participation in God's mission to the world (6, 9, 15, 36). While the document does not explicitly mention the homily, its almost thirty references to preaching the Word or preaching the Gospel make it clear that preaching is essential to the church fulfilling its responsibility to participate in God's mission to the world. The homily, as the central preaching act of the "source and summit" of the church's life must, therefore, be missiological by its very nature.

Liturgical Preaching as Participation in Missio Dei *(God's Mission)*

In other nascent ways, *FIYH* recognizes liturgical preaching as participating in God's mission. Multiple times, for example, it speaks of how communities of faith have the task of interpreting the world around them (10), are called to be witnesses to Christ in the world (10 and 43), and are enabled by a critical dialogue with contemporary culture (31) that calls believers to respond to the world (45). It also recognizes there are people struggling with a gospel response to economic oppression, world peace, and discrimination (74), and intimates the importance of having a "vision of the world."

In any future homiletic reflection, it will be important to assess the balance between the vision of a homily that looks "inside" to the baptized or "outside" to the world. Overall, the current document has a more centripetal than centrifugal image of the homily, which seems more intent on helping people make personal sense of their lives (e.g., 13–15, 48, 67, 68, 81, 107.5–6) than commissioning them for mission to the world. Thus, as noted above, there seems more concern with praise and thanks in this document than justice, ethics, or God's option for the poor.

The challenges in making the centrifugal turn in the homiletic act are multiple. One is coming to grips with the homily as an event that is not only preparatory for mission and preparing the baptized to carry out their witness in the Liturgy of the World but is also itself missiological. It participates in God's *missio*, embraces and upholds God's essential love for the world and not simply the church (cf. John 3:16), and does so with an unwavering ethical lens.

The Homily's Wider Public

A second challenge is the shifting demographics within Roman Catholic worshiping communities, in which there are many more unevangelized, seekers, and occasional worshipers coming to Sunday worship than there used to be. Thus, the missiological homily may be more about preevangelization or reevangelization than *FIYH* envisions (e.g., 42–43). This is particularly true in urban contexts and with young adults whom research suggests frequent Catholic worship sporadically and in decreased numbers.

A third challenge in thinking about the homily as missiological is recognizing that many hearers and interpreters of our preaching do not belong to the Roman Catholic church or even Christianity. Christian worship is ordinarily a publicized and open event, inviting not only the faithful but visitors and even skeptics to participate. Preaching to those present in the assembly, some worship is broadcast or recorded, some homilies are podcast or printed, and sometimes various aspects of our preaching are even commented on in the public press or excerpted on the internet. The homily, from this perspective, is an act of public theology that must communicate a vision of God's preemptive generosity and action in the world and how these are reflected in our church, worship, and belief to those who may know little about Catholicism or may be suspicious of our church. The more a homily is self-consciously shaped as a missiological dialogue with these wider publics—a dialogue well imaged in Vatican II's *Pastoral Constitution on the Church in the Modern World*—the more such a homily will participate effectively in God's mission, which is both its source and its goal.

IV. Methodology

Fred Baumer, Mary Margaret Pazdan, O.P.,
William Skudlarek, O.S.B., and Honora Werner, O.P.

Methodology in any discipline might be described as an anti-dote to myopia. Those who engage in creative work can become shortsighted and limit themselves to a narrow range of content, organization, and expression. An effective method provides creative practitioners with the ability to take a comprehensive look not only at what they are doing but also at how they are doing it, to make sure they are not omitting important steps in the creative process. The treatment of homiletic method presented in section 4 in *Fulfilled in Your Hearing* flows from its understanding of the Sunday assembly as an active participant in the liturgical celebration—including the preaching and its preparation—and not just a passive recipient (4, 7, 20, 106–8). A method designed to mine biblical and liturgical texts *only* for theological doctrines and ethical imperatives, much less good advice, is inappropriate for preaching.

The Methodology Proposed by Fulfilled in Your Hearing

When *FIYH* was published, significant changes were occurring in the discipline of homiletics that would influence preaching methodology in the coming years. Indeed, homileticians in the Protestant tradition in this country have been largely responsible for reinvigorating preaching and creating what has been called "the new homiletic." Fred Craddock's *One Without Authority* was formative in suggesting a shift from a deductive preaching model to an inductive one. Craddock, along with Edmund Steimle, Charles Rice, Morris Niedenthal, Eugene Lowry, and David Buttrick, to name a few, suggested a narrative preaching style that would be listener-centered and experiential and would proceed by way of image and story. An inductive homiletic method, then, allowed for the Sunday assembly to understand the Word of God from the horizon of their experience as active listeners.

The method described in section 4 of *FIYH* highlights the essentials of homily preparation, but does not set down a hard and fast model. Preachers are encouraged to become cognizant of the method they use most successfully in order to refine it and make it habitual (55) while also experimenting with new methods to keep their learning processes fresh and innovative. If any particular method was favored in the 1982 document, it is found in the recommendation that preachers begin their preparation by attending to the human situation evoked by the scriptural texts and then turn to the Scriptures to interpret how the God described in those texts is also actively present today (65).

Previous chapters in this commentary have already highlighted how consideration of the liturgical texts and ritual actions should also be included in the preparation process, taking into account what human experiences and hungers of the heart are being named and evoked by the prayers, hymns, sacred objects, and ritual actions of a particular liturgy. This final section will consider each of *FIYH*'s chapters insofar as method can be useful in the analysis of the assembly, the evaluation of the preacher, the exegesis of texts, and the process of writing the homily.

A Methodology for the Analysis of the Assembly

FIYH says that effective preaching depends on prayerful dwelling with the people as well as with the texts (11, 22). Preachers are urged to bring the concerns of the people in the assembly into dialogue with the texts (8, 9, 10, 32). The first question is: Who makes up the assembly? The first chapter here has already considered various ways of naming diversity through the "frames" of ethnicity, class, displacement, religious beliefs, and age cohorts. In this section we suggest a few steps that a preacher can take to assure that preaching takes this diversity into account.

Exegete the Entire Congregation

It is not hospitable for a preacher always to speak to the same group within the assembly, leaving the rest to "overhear" and then have to adjust the message to their own particular situation. An intentional awareness of the various groups must be a part of the preacher's method of preparation. Sometimes remarks will be particularly directed toward one or the other group, but over time, all groups should be deliberately included.

Homiletician Leonora Tubbs Tisdale indicates several areas on which the preacher might focus, such as the community's view(s) of God, their view(s) of humanity, and their view(s) of church (*Preaching as Local Theology*, 56–90). These points of view, shaped by culture, age, gender, and other factors, determine what a congregation will hear during the preaching. An assembly that has been formed with an image of God as a lawgiver who exacts high standards will hear language about God differently from one that has been formed with an image of God as a loving parent, quick to understand and forgive.

We would emphasize once again that preachers should also be encouraged to make use of various methods of "theological reflection," a pastoral practice that was not common in Roman Catholic theological education when *FIYH* was written. Employing such methods on a continuous basis will help form a habit of reflection as an integrating act.

Exegete the Physical Environment

Remember that the assembly and the parish are not identical. In addition to giving close attention to the assembly, preachers might consider the physical environment of the parish, that is, the physical settings that "house" the gathered assembly. This includes the physical plant. What does it say? "Fortress"? "Sacred space"? "Multipurpose building"? "McDonald's"? What do the grounds of the church communicate? How do such communication media as the parish bulletin and the parish web site reflect what the parish considers important? What is the experience of calling the parish office: How are you greeted and responded to? What do you listen to when you are put on hold? Such experiences communicate a sense of the parish where worship and preaching occur and play a part in shaping the assembly that comes to worship.

Exegete the Social Environment

The most effective way for a preacher to learn about a community is to frequent its gathering places and to accept invitations to homes and community celebrations. It can be very enlightening to work out a way to visit people at work to understand more fully what their work lives are like. Preachers also need to be aware of the level of unemployment in a community, the quality and need for health and daycare services, the accessibility of public transportation, and the other conditions that determine the quality of people's lives. There is a value, too, in reading the local and neighborhood papers and even such public documents as city council and school board minutes to have a sense of what is going on in the immediate environment. Alongside the connection people have with their civic community is the one they have with the larger church community; occasional references to what is happening in the diocese and in other dioceses throughout the world and within other faith communities, Christian and non-Christian, can deepen awareness of the assembly's link with the universal church and other religious groups.

On a more interpersonal level, take note of the topics and interests that most frequently come up in peoples' conversations and of the kinds of television programs and movies that capture their attention. By listening carefully, preachers will be able to identify the deep-seated beliefs and values of local congregations—beliefs and values that the people themselves may not be fully conscious of or able to articulate.

Finally, engaging in a group preparation method as suggested in *FIYH* that includes representatives of the various parish groups and subgroups will help preachers have a more refined sense of what people hear God saying to them in the Scriptures, the good news and challenges that are communicated in a particular set of readings.

A Methodology for the Evaluation of the Preacher

While section 2 of *FIYH* considered the identity, major tasks, and limitations of the preacher, there is a need today to focus more concretely on ways of providing ongoing evaluation, contributing to both the preacher's spiritual growth and development in the art and craft of homily presentation. It is never easy to receive critical evaluation, even though constructive feedback can improve one's ability to preach more effectively. Since preaching is such a personal act, homilists can feel personally threatened or put down when someone suggests their preaching would have been more effective had the content been altered by cutting something out or by changing the way something was said. But without such evaluation there is little likelihood of a change for the better.

Self-Evaluation

Perhaps the best way for preachers to begin is by taking an audio recorder into the pulpit or being unobtrusively recorded on a camcorder from the pew. They can then listen to or watch themselves to determine what might help their preaching become more authentic, intelligible, appealing, and inspiring. Four focus areas come to mind for evaluation that assists growth:

    a) Regarding the Assembly: Did the stories, references, and language used in preaching make it obvious that the homily was shaped for this people, at this time, in this place? Do the examples demonstrate a broad appeal to different segments of the assembly, rather than reflecting the life experience of only one or two subgroups?

b) Regarding the Texts: Did the preaching flow out of prayerful reflection on the scriptural and liturgical texts, or was it loosely connected by only a word or phrase? Did the text end up being a pretext for the personal agenda of the preacher?

c) Regarding the Preacher: Was there a "so what" for the preacher as part of the preparation, so that the preacher's spirituality was engaged and even challenged? Was the preacher's engagement with the material evident during the presentation?

d) Regarding the Communication Dynamics: Was there an engaging opening, a coherent flow of thought, a cohesive structure, a pointed conclusion? Was there vocal energy, "person contact" (not just darting eye contact), an appropriate length? Was there vocal variety, sufficient volume, fitting emotional expression? Was the pace too slow, too fast, too much the same? Did it sound conversational or more like a detached reading?

Community and Peer Evaluation

Evaluation may be done more profitably with several members of the assembly who were present, or by peers who gather a few days later to view a video of the preaching. A number of resources describe how an evaluation can be structured, but the real challenge is for preachers to make it a priority and initiate an evaluation process. Formation programs for preachers need to emphasize how essential evaluation is to good preaching and provide future preachers with suggestions about how to do it. *FIYH* does not suggest any particular evaluation method, but two possibilities come to mind:

a) Periodically ask listeners to respond to two questions on an index card handed out randomly at the beginning of worship:

1. What did the preacher say to you? (in a sentence)

2. What would you affirm about the preacher's presentation? What would you recommend—one suggestion for content, one suggestion for preaching style?

The first question will give direct feedback to the preacher on content, particularly on what was heard in relation to what the preacher wanted to be heard. The second will give a listener's more personal reaction to both content and style.

b) For a more in-depth evaluation, the four focus areas mentioned above in the preacher's self-evaluation could also be used by a group of parishioners or fellow preachers.

The epilogue of *FIYH* refers to the image of the carved handrail leading up the steps of St. Stephen's medieval pulpit in Vienna, Austria, with its ugly mythical creatures, their open mouths and threatening jaws reminding the preacher of his personal weaknesses and sinfulness as he climbed ever higher. At the very top of the steps facing these threatening figures, however, was a barking dog, whose open jaws indicated that these hellish creatures had no hope of entering the sacred place of preaching. The preacher was to leave behind a preoccupation with his sinful self and preach God's word humbly, honestly, and lovingly. A disciplined approach to preaching evaluation can help this to happen.

A Methodology for Studying the Biblical Texts

FIYH was written at a time when the full flowering of the historical-critical method of interpreting Scripture had occurred and so it gave emphasis to this approach to studying the texts by focusing on the author's intention and what the text meant for its original audience. This method often tended toward an exegesis-application approach in preaching preparation, with the preacher offering a word on what it meant then and how we could apply it now. Certainly the historical-critical method continues to make an important contribution to understanding the biblical texts. It alone, however, is not adequate for preaching. More needs to be done than exegeting the text for its past meaning and then applying that meaning to today. What is needed today is a hermeneutic approach that includes contemporary methods of interpretation and communication. In this way, the focus of the preacher's study is on "the present meaning mediated by language through interpretation rather than in historical meanings uncovered by exegesis which are then inserted into contemporary contexts by a process of application" (Schneiders, 1990, 1160). Past meanings do not exhaust the understanding of any text.

Furthermore, it is significant that biblical texts are in a lectionary. The use of a lectionary directs attention to the principle of *lectio continua* that guided the choice of scriptural texts in the lectionary (85), providing a sense of continuity both with what has preceded and what will follow. The lectionary also makes room for the meaning that can arise when diverse texts are placed next to each other and enter into dialogue with each other. Preachers should carefully read and reread all four lectionary texts aloud—including the responsorial psalm, in Greek/ Hebrew if possible, in different translations, and in their biblical context—all the while jotting down first responses, questions, reactions while reading (86, 87, 88). Reading texts aloud can help a preacher to hear the scriptural words as "real," spoken to actual people, at a particular time, in a certain place. This imaginative, interpretive action is more likely to lead to a preaching event that helps an assembly, preacher and people alike, to encounter God now (53–54). Along with this attentive reading of the biblical texts, there should also be an attentive reading of all the other liturgical texts.

A Spiral Process of Preparation

A spiral process can include prayer, reading, meditation, contemplation, study, and, finally, proclamation. Throughout the process there is dialogue due to a continuous return to prayer, meditation, and contemplation, allowing for new connections and insight, before the preaching takes place. Prayer, meditation, and contemplation are at the heart of preaching. While study of the biblical texts is essential, preachers should beware of relying solely on the scholarship of others, much less on the finished product of another. Prayerful reflection on the texts must precede and accompany study (89, 90, 91). Prayer and meditation include reflecting on our relationships with God, others (especially the assembly), the cosmos, and self in light of these texts. In praying specifically with lectionary texts in a particular liturgical season, preachers grow in awareness of how the Spirit directs them to listen for connections—a word, an image, a symbol, a gesture—appropriate to the season. The value of engaging in *lectio divina*, both individually and as a community, has already been highly recommended (see Dysinger). The questions that arise from our prayerful contemplation of the texts can lead us to a more focused study when we dialogue with biblical interpreters (see Van Harn, *The Lectionary Commentary*; *The New Interpreters Bible Handbook of Preaching*; *The Text This Week* [http://www.textweek.com]).

The Three Worlds of Biblical Interpretation

Ordinarily, questions regarding the Scriptures are related to the three worlds of biblical interpretation. The *world behind the text* has been the focus of two methods: the historical-critical and the social-scientific. Both methods are author-centered, focusing on how a particular writer communicated to persons of a past time with worldviews different from today. The social-scientific method is a newer discipline that studies patterns of culture and human behavior in the Mediterranean world. If questions arise about how persons then lived with one another—their values and moral and social codes—about issues of anthropology, and by what means the message of a particular book would have been heard, historical criticism and social-scientific criticism are needed.

The *world of the text* receives the attention of literary and rhetorical criticism. Both methods are text-centered, allowing preachers to enter into the world of the text itself, the story being told, the characters presented, and to examine the truth contained within the text without attention to outer historical circumstances. The focus is on the intricacies of the text itself. If questions concern setting, characters, plot, structure, or the arrangement of words and phrases, literary criticism is useful (see Bergant and Fragemini, Puskas, Lammers Gross).

The *world in front of the text* is the focus of reader-response criticism, attending to today's readers of a text and often rooted in an advocacy position toward a specific group, e.g., those addressed by liberationist, feminist, or postcolonial criticism. Since each position is contextualized locally, i.e., for this group, at this time, in this place, any generalization of the method is not adequate. Preachers may find themselves taking up one of these perspectives on behalf of a particular congregation or a group within the congregation. Nonetheless, to know diverse assemblies through social analysis and study, a commentary that relates to at least one such group requires specific effort, e.g., an African-American liberation interpretation (see Felder). If questions relate specifically to the needs, interests, pain, or hope of a particular group in our assembly, some form of reader-response criticism is a place to start.

The three worlds of biblical criticism are distinct, yet interrelated. Questions arising from prayer and contemplation may lead to one or more of them. Consistent prayer, study, and dialogue with others are partners for preaching. In moving from prayer to study, preachers may experience a distancing, a separation, even a disconnection between them. But such movement can help one to become aware of various presuppositions and worldviews consciously or unconsciously held. Biblical interpreters can be invaluable dialogue partners. Sometimes the article that occasions the most struggle provides a strong foundation for preaching. Going back to prayer to ask the Spirit for assistance can lead to preaching from the heart. Being faithful to the method that moves us from prayer to reading the text to prayer to study of the text to prayer, etc.—and doing this for all the texts, biblical and liturgical—gives birth to a proclamation of a new creation for the present time. Then preaching becomes a fusion of prayer, study, and dialogue that is personal, Spirit-filled, and truly directed to a particular assembly.

A Methodology for Developing the Homily

The Use of Homily Preparation Groups, Homily Services, and the Internet

FIYH asserts that preachers need to devote adequate time to preparation and to spread this preparation time over the course of a week rather than into a few hours the evening before preaching (21, 82, 83). It recommends the use of a homily preparation group, composed either of fellow preachers or of other members of the assembly. A method for group preparation focuses on the human experiences evoked by the texts within those who have gathered (20, 108). While FIYH speaks in terms of face-to-face meetings, members of the assembly or fellow preachers can now be invited into a virtual space to share their reflections on the texts.

Noting the homily services that existed in the early eighties, FIYH wisely observes that, while these could never replace the preacher's own prayer, study, and work, they could be helpful, if they were attentive to the principles of continuity and harmony on which the lectionary is based and if they provided preachers with examples and illustrations enabling a particular text to be heard as God's word to the church today (59). Today, resources far more extensive and accessible than homily services of the past are available through the internet. Preachers have at their fingertips a treasury of exegetical, theological, hermeneutic, homiletic, liturgical, literary, and artistic riches that, in the past, would have been available only to those with access to a large research library.

The web also offers examples of homilies that reveal the many different ways preachers hear God's living, comforting, challenging Word for the gathered faithful. Preachers can benefit from listening to or reading the texts of other preachers, both discovering what others found to be the connecting link between peoples' concerns and the Word of God in the Sunday's Scriptures, and then observing how they crafted a preaching text that helps people hear God inviting them into a deeper and more life-giving relationship. Reading or hearing the preaching of others or their ideas for preaching can help us imagine how

God's Word can continue to find expression through a preacher's imagination, experience, and stories.

Preachers must, of course, exercise good judgment in deciding which resources to use, as well as what use to make of them in their preaching. Simply downloading someone else's preaching text and delivering it as one's own is a gross violation of professional ethics. To do so would be dishonest. While it is true that we have nothing that we have not received (see 1 Cor 4:7) and that every preaching event, no matter how much prayer, study, and work went into it, depends on a word we have received and refashioned, still the honest preacher will give credit whenever use is made of another's insight, image, or story.

Some preachers have posted their preaching texts for parishioners unable to be present for the Sunday celebration. While reading a text online is often a pale substitute for participating in the liturgy and experiencing the preacher in the present moment, still the availability of a homily given for a congregation living in today's circumstances can be greatly welcomed by parishioners in the military, away at college, or confined by sickness or frailty.

Method and Writing

At some point in the preparation process, writing out one's thoughts can help to move the homily toward a clear focus and structure. The physical act of jotting down ideas and then writing out a rough draft of a manuscript remains an essential early step for many as they prepare to preach. Write "without the brakes on," putting down whatever comes to mind. The first draft should bring the preacher to the point of knowing what the message is (in a sentence) and its purpose (in a sentence), that is, the focus and function of the message. Revising and editing comes later. This is the time to settle on what to say, the sequence of thought, and including material that appeals to the mind and the heart. Paying special attention to whatever in the texts may evoke resistance or puzzlement within the preacher can often lead to a surprising and deep engagement with the word of God.

Some preachers are afraid that if they write out what they are going to preach, they will lose spontaneity and immediacy when it comes time to preach. Their fear comes from a mistaken identification between writing and reading. *FIYH* insists that homilies need to be written, but quickly adds that they should not be read; at the very least, they should not *sound* read (104, 105). It is possible to read a text and sound perfectly spontaneous, provided the text was intentionally prepared to be spoken by being written in an oral style. So, during the writing stage, the preacher writes in a conversational style. And in the presentation stage, the preacher engages in active and present thinking and feeling, being present to what is being said as it is being said.

Following this initial draft, walk away from what has been done. Leave it for a while. Allow for an incubation period, let things "cook" on their own, outside of one's conscious attention. By getting some distance from it, it is possible to see it with fresh eyes and hear it anew on returning to it. Think of it as allowing time for the Holy Spirit to work (92, 93). After looking at it a second time, it is time to edit and cut or edit and add. The work of editing allows for the following:

1) to make the language of the homily more conversational (63, 97)

2) to be sure that transitions are clear and make sense (98)

3) to give special attention to the introduction and conclusion (98)

4) to make certain that the focus of the homily is unambiguous (99)

5) to ensure that the preaching is integral to the liturgical celebration, helping the community to move into liturgy, and then motivating them for some aspect of mission (100)

Skilled preachers write a text precisely to make sure that what they want to say will sound natural and be clear to the listener on first hearing. They write out a text because it is easier to discover and eliminate clichés, abstractions, and jargon. Also, writing is a way of making sure that the preaching begins and ends effectively. Some preachers find it hard to take off; others, to land. Homilies rarely spring full grown out of a preacher's head but come to a satisfactory state only through writing and rewriting. Word processing has proven to be such a boon to preachers. In the days of pens and typewriters, many preachers had neither the time nor the energy to rewrite what they had put down on paper. Thanks to computer technology, inserting a more appropriate word or phrase or rearranging or cutting whole paragraphs can be done with ease. When preparing, preachers have an easier time moving from noncritical exposition ("writing without the brakes on") to analytic assessment (editing). Both actions are necessary in the creative process, but, as *FIYH* emphasized, they need to happen in separate stages (96, 97).

Method and Delivery

Delivering a message does not begin when the preacher stands before the assembly. *FIYH* urges the preacher to practice aloud and to ask for feedback before going into the pulpit (101). Some preachers record their preaching in advance so they can listen to it beforehand. With today's digital video cameras, preachers can easily see as well as hear themselves by simply downloading the digital file to their computers. As for preaching with or without notes or a manuscript, *FIYH* favors whatever practice allows for greater freedom, authenticity, clarity, and "staying on point." It does emphasize, however, the importance of facial expression and bodily movement in preaching (102–5), which can be diminished, if not lost, when a text is read.

Educators and communications experts note that modern technology affects the assembly's perception. People really do hear and see differently than they did twenty-five years ago. The preacher needs to take this development into account, especially now that exclusively oral public communication is becoming less common. For many, public communication is more effective when the spoken word is accompanied by images and outlines projected on a screen. The preacher may not be comfortable with the use of such technology, but if so many of the assembly prefer and even need visual images, preachers may need to step out of their comfort zone. At the same time, they must be sensitive to the fact that some in the assembly may react negatively to the introduction of modern communication technology in preaching: "Oh no! Not another PowerPoint presentation!"

Some would argue that liturgy abhors what is artificial and contrived, and, therefore, technology has no place there because it is a form of "virtual reality." Yet, microphones, electronic organs and keyboards, and, in an earlier age, many musical instruments were slow to be accepted in liturgical celebrations because they were identified with secular entertainment. Perhaps part of the reason the use of modern media technology in preaching and the liturgy is problematic for some people is because of this identification with popular entertainment.

If technologies such as PowerPoint or audio and visual media are brought into the liturgy, they will best be employed to supplement and enhance the preacher's voice, not to replace the heartfelt words of a person of faith speaking within the assembly (39). Media also need to be employed in such a way that it is clear that the purpose is not to entertain but to enhance communication. At the same time, just because people experience liturgy and preaching as enjoyable is not necessarily an indication that they are coming only to be entertained. The use of technology in preaching and in the liturgy remains a subject of discussion. Further study and experimentation will help clarify how and when it is appropriate. Its use within the liturgy will always require skill and sensitivity.

A further issue that may need greater attention is that of the availability and accessibility to technology being limited only to the more financially well-off parishes and worship sites. This is an ethical issue that is likely to become more important as technological development becomes more sophisticated.

FIYH concludes its treatment of homiletic methodology by reiterating the non-negotiables of good preparation for preaching: time, prayer, study, organization, concreteness, and evaluation (111). These hold as true today as when the document was written. Are there others to be added for our own time?

A Final Word

At the present and for the foreseeable future the preacher's greatest legacy to those who gather for worship is language. Preachers should offer words that evoke, express, and deepen faith. They hope to nourish people hungry for both a vision that illuminates and a message that nourishes. Given that words are such frail things, carried on the breath, present only for the moment, then evaporating beyond reach, even so, if we manage to put the right ones in the right order, minds can be opened, hearts transformed, and wills moved to work to bring about the kingdom of God. In bringing this commentary to a close, we express the hope that it will help to renew an appreciation for what *Fulfilled in Your Hearing* attempted to achieve over twenty-five years ago: to provide a vision of and enthusiasm for liturgical preaching that would energize preachers and affect the lives of listeners, drawing all into a deeper union with Christ and each other, whenever we join together to give glory to the Father through the Son in the Spirit. When preaching manages to achieve this, it truly becomes a word that is "fulfilled in our hearing."

Appendix A

Fulfilled in Your Hearing

The Homily in the Sunday Assembly

Bishops' Committee on Priestly Life and Ministry

United States Conference of Catholic Bishops

15 February 1982

Introduction

"The primary duty of priests is the proclamation of the Gospel of God to all." These clear, straightforward words of the Second Vatican Council (*Decree on the Ministry and Life of Priests*, #4) may still come as something of a surprise to us. We might more spontaneously think that the primary duty of priests is the celebration of the Church's sacraments, or the pastoral care of the People of God, or the leadership of a Christian community. Yet the words of the document are clear: the proclamation of the Gospel is primary. The other duties of the priest are to be considered properly presbyteral to the degree that they support the proclamation of the Gospel.

"Proclamation" can cover a wide variety of activities in the church. A life of quiet faith and generous loving deeds is proclamation; the celebration of the Eucharist is the proclamation "of the death of the Lord until he comes." But a key moment in the proclamation of the Gospel is preaching, preaching which is characterized by "proclamation of God's wonderful works in the history of salvation, that is, the mystery of Christ, which is ever made present and active within us, especially in the celebration of the liturgy" (*Constitution on the Sacred Liturgy*, #35, 2).

The Decree on the Ministry and Life of Priests is especially clear in relating the ministry of preaching to that of the celebration of the sacraments. Since these sacraments are sacraments of faith, and since "faith is born of the Word and nourished by it," the preaching of the Word is an essential part of the celebration of the sacraments. This is especially true in the celebration of the Eucharist, the document goes on to note, for "in this celebration the proclamation of the death and resurrection of the Lord is inseparably joined both to the response of the people who hear, and to the very offering whereby Christ ratified the New Testament in His blood."

This intimate link between preaching and the celebration of the sacraments, especially of the Sunday Eucharist, is what we intend to address in this document on preaching. We recognize that preaching is not limited to priests. Deacons are also ordained ministers of the Word. Indeed, the proclamation of the Word of God is the responsibility of the entire Christian community by virtue of the sacrament of baptism. Moreover, we recognize that preaching is not limited to the Eucharist, and we are pleased to support the ways in which more and more Catholics are celebrating the power of God's Word in evangelistic gatherings, in the catechumenate, and in groups devoted to the study of the Bible and to prayer. We also recognize that for the vast majority of Catholics the Sunday homily is the normal and frequently the formal way in which they hear the Word of God proclaimed. For these Catholics the Sunday homily may well be the most decisive factor in determining the depth of their faith and strengthening the level of their commitment to the church.

The focus of this document, therefore, will be the Sunday homily, and even more specifically, the homily preached by the bishop or priest who presides at the celebration of the Eucharist. Again, we recognize that there are occasions when the homily may be preached by someone other than the presider, by a deacon serving in the parish or a guest priest preacher, for example. Yet, in terms of common practice and of liturgical norm, the preaching of the homily belongs to the presiding minister. (See *The General Instruction of the Roman Missal*, #42: "The homily should ordinarily be given by the celebrant.") The unity of Word and Sacrament is thus symbolized in the person of the presiding minister of the Eucharist.

While this document is addressed specifically to priests who have a pastoral ministry that involves regular Sunday preaching, we hope that all who are concerned with effective proclamation of the Gospel will find it helpful. This document may also prove useful in the preparation for and continuing formation of permanent deacons as ministers of the Word.

We propose that this document be used as a basis of discussion among priests and bishops, and by priests with members of their congregations. In such sharing of personal experiences, of expectations and frustrations, and by mutual support, we find hope for a renewal of preaching in the church today.

I. *The Assembly*

[1] Jesus came to Nazareth where he had been reared, and entering the synagogue on the sabbath as he was in the habit of doing, he stood up to do the reading. When the book of the prophet Isaiah was handed him, he unrolled the scroll and found the passage where it was written:

> "The spirit of the Lord is upon me;
>   therefore he has anointed me.
> He has sent me to bring glad tidings to the poor,
>   to proclaim liberty to captives,
> Recovery of sight to the blind
>   and release to prisoners,
> To announce a year of favor from the Lord."

Rolling up the scroll he gave it back to the assistant and sat down. All in the synagogue had their eyes fixed on him. Then he began by saying to them, "Today this Scripture passage is fulfilled in your hearing." All who were present spoke favorably of him; they marveled at the appealing discourse which came from his lips. (Lk 4:14–22a)

[2] These verses from the fourth chapter of the Gospel of Saint Luke present us with a picture of Jesus as reader and homilist in the synagogue at Nazareth. He stands up to read the lesson from the prophet which was placed at the end of the service. He then draws on this passage to speak to the here-and-now situation. All who listened to him were favorably impressed.

[3] The three major elements of liturgical preaching are all here: the preacher, the word drawn from the Scriptures, and the gathered community. Each element is essential and each must be considered carefully if we are to understand the challenge and the possibilities of liturgical preaching.

[4] We believe that it is appropriate, indeed essential, to begin this treatment of the Sunday homily with the assembly rather than with the preacher or the homily, and this for two principal reasons. First of all we can point to the great emphasis which

communication theorists place on an accurate understanding of the audience if communication is to be effective. Unless a preacher knows what a congregation needs, wants, or is able to hear, there is every possibility that the message offered in the homily will not meet the needs of the people who hear it. To say this is by no means to imply that preachers are only to preach what their congregations want to hear. Only when preachers know what their congregations want to hear will they be able to communicate what a congregation needs to hear. Homilists may indeed preach on what they understand to be the real issues, but if they are not in touch with what the people think are the real issues, they will very likely be misunderstood or not heard at all. What is communicated is not what is said, but it is what is heard, and what is heard is determined in large measure by what the hearer needs or wants to hear.[1]

[5] Contemporary ecclesiology provides a second and even more fundamental reason for beginning with the assembly rather than with the preacher or the homily. *The Dogmatic Constitution on the Church* describes the church as the mystery of God's saving will, given concrete historical expression in the people with whom he has entered into a covenant. This church is the visible sacrament of the saving unity to which God calls all people. "Established by Christ as a fellowship of life, charity, and truth, the church is also used by Him as an instrument for the redemption of all, and is sent forth into the whole world as the light of the world and the salt of the earth" (#9). The church, therefore, is first and foremost a gathering of those whom the Lord has called into a covenant of peace with himself. In this gathering, as in every other, offices and ministries are necessary, but secondary. The primary reality is Christ in the assembly, the People of God.

[6] This renewed understanding of the church is gradually becoming consciously present in the words and actions of the Catholic people. By means of their involvement in diocesan and parish organizations, their sharing in various forms of ministry, and their active participation in the liturgy, they are beginning to

experience what it means to say that the people are the church and the church are people.

[7] Obviously the development we are speaking of is not uniform. But it is clear that the parish in which the priest acts in an arbitrary manner, in which virtually all active ministry—liturgical, educational, and social—is in the hands of the clergy and religious, and in which the laity do little more than attend Mass and receive the sacraments, is no longer the norm. Such a drastic change in the practices and self-consciousness of the Catholic congregation is bound to have significant consequences for the content and style of preaching that takes place in the Sunday Eucharistic assembly.

To preach in a way that sounds as if the preacher alone has access to the truth and knows what is best for everyone else, or that gives the impression that there are no unresolved problems or possibility for dialogue, is to preach in a way that may have been acceptable to those who viewed the church primarily in clerical terms. In a church that thinks and speaks of itself as a pilgrim people, gathered together for worship, witness, and work, such preaching will be heard only with great difficulty, if at all.

The Identity of the Assembly

[8] The Eucharistic assembly that gathers Sunday after Sunday is a rich and complex phenomenon. Even in parishes that are more or less uniform in ethnic, social, or economic background, there is great diversity: men and women, old and young, the successes and the failures, the joyful and the bereaved, the fervent and the halfhearted, the strong and the weak. Such diversity is a constant challenge to the preacher, for our words can all too easily be heard as excluding one or the other segment of the congregation. We may not mean to ignore the presence of women when we say "Jesus came to save all men," but if exclusion is heard, then exclusion is communicated, whether intended or not.

[9] While the diversity of every assembly is a factor that needs to be taken seriously by the preacher, and all the more so when

the diversity cuts across racial, ethnic, economic, and social lines, this diversity should not blind us to another, even greater reality: the unity of the congregation. This assembly has come together because its members have been baptized into the one body of Christ and share a common faith. This faith, though rooted in a common baptismal identity, is expressed in ways that extend from the highest levels of personal appropriation and intellectual understanding to the most immature forms of ritualism and routine. And yet, to a greater or lesser degree, it is faith in Jesus Christ that is common to all the members of a community gathered for Eucharist.

[10] To say that a community shares a common faith is to say that its members have a common way of interpreting the world around them. For the Christian community, the world is seen and interpreted as the creation of a loving God. Although this world turned away from God through sin, God reached out again and again to draw the world to himself, finally sending his own Son in human flesh. This Son expressed the fullness of the Father's love by accepting death on the cross. The Father in turn glorified his Son by raising him from the dead and making him the source of eternal life for all who believe. Believers witness to the presence and word of Jesus in the world and are a continuing sign of the Kingdom of God, which is present both in and through Jesus, and still to come to its fullness through the power of the Holy Spirit.

[11] In very broad outline this is the common faith that binds together the Christian community gathering for worship. No individual in the community would very likely express the faith in quite these words. Some might find it difficult to express their faith in any words at all. They do not possess the background of theology to enable them to do so. We might say, therefore, that one of the principal tasks of the preacher is to provide the congregation of the faithful with words to express their faith, and with words to express the human realities to which this faith responds. Through words drawn from the Scriptures, from the church's theological tradition, and from the personal appropriation of that tradition through study and prayer, the preacher

joins himself and the congregation in a common vision. We ca..
say, therefore, that the homily is a unifying moment in the celebration of the liturgy, deepening and giving expression to the
unity that is already present through the sacrament of baptism.

The Preacher as Mediator of Meaning

[12] The person who preaches in the context of the liturgical
assembly is thus a mediator, representing both the community
and the Lord. The assembly gathers for liturgy as a community
of faith, believing that God has acted in human history and
more particularly, in their own history. The community gathers
to respond to this living and active God. They may also gather
to question how or whether the God who once acted in human
history is still present and acting today. They may wonder how
this God, whom the Scriptures present as so powerful and so
loving, can be experienced in lives today that seem so broken
and meaningless. How can parents believe in a God who raises
the dead to life when their daughter has just been killed in a car
accident? How can a family hope in a God who leads his people
out of slavery into freedom when they are trapped in an infla-
tionary spiral in which costs increase and the buying power of
their salaries diminishes? How can young people join with the
angels and saints in praise of the glory of God when they are
struggling with the challenges of establishing their own identi-
ties and their relationship to family and friends?

[13] The preacher represents this community by voicing its concerns, by naming its demons, and thus enabling it to gain some
understanding and control of the evil which afflicts it. He represents the Lord by offering the community another word, a word
of healing and pardon, of acceptance and love. Like humans
everywhere, the people who make up the liturgical assembly
are people hungry, sometimes desperately so, for meaning in
their lives. For a time they may find meaning in their jobs, their
families and friends, their political or social causes. All these
concerns, good and valid as they are, fall short of providing
ultimate meaning. Without ultimate meaning, we are ultimately

unsatisfied. If we are able to hear a word which gives our lives another level of meaning, which interprets them in relation to God, then our response is to turn to this source of meaning in an attitude of praise and thanksgiving.

[14] The community that gathers Sunday after Sunday comes together to offer God praise and thanksgiving, or at least to await a word that will give a meaning to their lives and enable them to celebrate Eucharist. What the preacher can do best of all at this time and in this place is to enable this community to celebrate by offering them a word in which they can recognize their own concerns and God's concern for them.

[15] The preacher acts as a mediator, making connections be-tween the real lives of people who believe in Jesus Christ but are not always sure what difference faith can make in their lives, and the God who calls us into ever deeper communion with himself and with one another. Especially in the Eucharistic celebration, the sign of God's saving presence among his people, the preacher is called to point to the signs of God's presence in the lives of his people so that, in joyous recognition of that presence, they may join the angels and saints to proclaim God's glory and sing with them their unending hymn of praise.

II. The Preacher

[16] We began our treatment of the Sunday homily by looking first to the assembly that gathers to celebrate the liturgy of the Eucharist. Such a beginning could be interpreted to mean that the importance of the ordained priesthood is not what it used to be. Nothing could be further from the truth. The priesthood of the faithful and the ordained ministerial priesthood although distinct are not opposed to one another. In fact, they stand or fall together. To the degree that we give full weight to the priesthood of all the baptized, to that degree do we see the full importance and significance of the ordained priesthood. To the degree that we downplay the importance of the priesthood of the faithful, to that degree is the ordained priesthood diminished.

[17] The community gathered to worship is a priestly people, men and women called to offer God worship. If this community is conscious of its dignity, then those it calls to service in positions of leadership will be able to recognize their dignity as well. We think of the priest as the representative of Christ. This way of thinking is true, as long as we remember that one represents Christ by representing the church, for the church is the fundamental sacrament of Christ. Moreover, it is the church, through its bishops, that calls individuals to presbyteral ministry in the church.

Pastoral Role of the Preacher

[18] Preachers who are conscious of their representative role strive to preach in a way that indicates they know and identify with the people to whom they are speaking. Their preaching is pastoral, displaying a sensitive and concerned knowledge of the struggles, doubts, concerns, and joys of the members of a local community.

[19] To be in touch with the cares and concerns, needs and good fortunes of the assembly does not mean that the preacher has to answer questions or solve problems in every homily. There will be occasions when nothing we can say will do anything to change a situation. We cannot raise a dead daughter to life; our words will not stop inflation or lower unemployment. What our words can do is help people make connections between the realities of their lives and the realities of the Gospel. We can help them see how God in Jesus Christ has entered and identified himself with the human realities of pain and of happiness.

Listening and Praying

[20] In order to make such connections between the lives of the people and the Gospel, the preacher will have to be a listener before he is a speaker. Listening is not an isolated moment. It is a way of life. It means openness to the Lord's voice not only in the Scriptures but in the events of our daily lives and in the

experience of our brothers and sisters. It is not just *my* listening but *our* listening together for the Lord's word to the community. We listen to the Scriptures, we listen to the people, and we ask, "What are they saying to one another? What are they asking of one another?" And out of that dialogue between the Word of God in the Scriptures and the Word of God in the lives of his people, the Word of God in preaching begins to take shape.

[21] Attentive listening to the Scriptures and to the people is, in essence, a form of prayer, perhaps the form of prayer most appropriate to the spirituality of the priest and preacher. There is nothing more essential than prayerful listening for effective preaching, a praying over the texts which seeks the light and fire of the Holy Spirit to kindle the *now* meaning in our hearts. A week of daily meditation on the readings of the following Sunday is not too much time to spend in preparation for the preaching we are called to do on the Lord's Day. Such regular preparation will allow us not only to savor the word in prayer but also to incorporate the experiences of a full week into our preparation.

[22] Such extended, prayerful preparation is so important for preaching because it helps us reach the moment of inspiration, an inspiration that has affinities to poetic inspiration but is more. We ask for and expect the real movement of the Holy Spirit in us and in the assembly. If the words of Scripture are divinely inspired, as we believe them to be, then divine inspiration must be at work when those words are made alive and contemporary to the believing community in and through our ministry.

[23] The preacher is thus called, above all, to be prayerful. The prayer we speak of is not prayer alongside of preparation for preaching, or over and above this preparation, but the very heart and center of the preparation itself. Unless the Word of God in the Scriptures is interiorized through prayerful study and reflection, it cannot possibly sustain the life-giving, love-generating words that preachers want to offer their people. Preachers then are called to a prayerful dwelling with their people and to a

prayerful dwelling with the texts of Scripture knowing them and allowing themselves to be known by them.

[24] This dwelling with the Scriptures and with the people which is the necessary prelude to effective preaching points to the necessity for certain pastoral skills and academic knowledge, both of which the modern seminary offers its candidates for priesthood, but which need continual updating and refining. We speak here of the skills of understanding and communicating with people, and of the knowledge required for the accurate and relevant interpretation of Scriptural texts.

Interpreting the Scriptures

[25] Let us begin with the second requirement first, since that is somewhat easier to describe. The interpretation of texts is the science of hermeneutics, and in order to accomplish its end, hermeneutics relies first of all on exegesis. For exegesis to be done at the highest professional level, the exegete must have knowledge of the original languages, access to the tools of textual criticism, extensive historical and archeological background, a comprehensive knowledge of the development of biblical faith, and a familiarity with the history of the theological interpretation of texts in both the synagogue and the Christian churches. Obviously few preachers have the training or access to the resources for exegesis of this kind.

[26] Exegesis for preaching need not always be done at the highest professional level. Our seminary training and our continuing education provide us with tools and resources to tap the best of contemporary exegesis in a fruitful way. Even a smattering of Hebrew and Greek is helpful in capturing the flavor or nuances of certain words. An acquaintance with the methods of scriptural scholarship enables us to understand, for example, why the sayings of Jesus can appear in such different contexts, and therefore with such different meanings, in the Gospels. Or again, knowing how the biblical author used a particular passage as a building block in a larger literary context can help us appreciate how the

church of succeeding ages found it important to set the passage in contemporary contexts, a task which is ours in the liturgical celebration today.

[27] It is hard to imagine that a person who has as his primary duty the proclamation of the Gospel to all would be without the basic tools and methods that help to ensure an accurate understanding of this Gospel. Surely every preacher ought to have a basic library to turn to in the preparation of homilies. A good Bible dictionary will help in picturing the background of a passage; a concordance will locate other passages that are related; a "theological" dictionary of Scripture will trace ideas that recur through Old and New Testaments; Gospel parallels will set similar texts that occur in more than one Gospel side by side. Standard commentaries on the major books of the Bible that appear in the lectionary should also be ready at hand, as well as exegetical commentaries based on the lectionary itself.

[28] The texts of Scripture from which our preaching flows are not locked in antiquity. They are texts which have nourished the church's life throughout all its history, sustaining it in times of trial, calling it back to fidelity in times of weakness and opening up new possibilities when it seemed immobilized by the weight of human traditions.

[29] The history of the interpretation of the Scriptures is part of the contemporary meaning of the Scriptures. The way they have been preached, the liturgical expressions they have generated, the prayer they have nourished, the magisterial statements they have inspired, the theological systems they have fostered, even the heresies they have occasioned, expand and deepen the way the Scriptures speak to us today.

[30] It is the faith of the church that the preacher must proclaim, not merely his own. Consequently, the more familiar the preacher is with the history of scriptural interpretation and the development of the church's doctrine, the more capable he is of bringing that word into dialogue with the contemporary situation. Church doctrine is nourished by profound meditation upon

the inspired Word, the exegesis of the fathers, conciliar documents and the teaching of the Magisterium. Therefore, the qualified preacher will lead his people to ever greater unity of faith among themselves as well as with prior generations of believers.

[31] It is somewhat more difficult to speak of what is involved in the understanding of people and how the priest/preacher can prepare himself for this demand of his office. Surely part of the rationale of the requirement that students in theological seminaries have a background in the liberal arts, with an emphasis on philosophy, is that familiarity with the leading ideas, movements, and personalities of human civilization (or at least of Western civilization) will enable preachers to engage in a critical dialogue with contemporary culture, recognizing what is conformable with the Gospel, challenging that which is not. The great artistic and literary achievements of a culture are surely a privileged means of access to the heart and mind of a people.

[32] Regular and sustained contact with the world's greatest literature or with its painting, sculpture, and musical achievements can rightfully be regarded by preachers not simply as a leisure time activity but as part of their ongoing professional development. The same can be said of attention to modern entertainment media—television, film, radio—or to the theater. Dramatic presentations that deal sensitively with significant human issues can provide a wealth of material for our reflection and our preaching, both in its content and in its form.

[33] If preachers are to know and understand their congregations today, some familiarity with popular forms of entertainment may also be necessary. We need not spend whole afternoons watching soap operas, memorizing baseball statistics, or listening to the latest hit albums. Yet if we are totally unaware, or give the impression that we are unaware of the activities and interests to which people devote a good deal of their leisure time, energy, and money, it will be difficult for us to make connections between their lives and the Gospel, or to call them to fuller, richer, and deeper levels of faith response.

[34] Finally, preachers need to devote some time and energy to understanding the complex social, political, and economic forces that are shaping the contemporary world. Watching the evening news on television or scanning the headlines of the daily paper may be a beginning but it is not enough. Preachers need exposure to more serious and sustained commentary on the contemporary world, the kind of exposure that can be gained through a program of reading or through conversation with people who are professionally involved in such areas as business, politics, or medicine. Without this kind of informed understanding of the complex world we live in, preaching too easily degenerates into platitudes of faith, meaningless broadsides against the wickedness of the modern world, or into an uncritical affirmation of the wonderful advances that have taken place in modern times.

[35] To have a comprehensive knowledge of the social, political and economic forces shaping the contemporary world, while at the same time specializing in scriptural exegesis and theology and being pastorally competent may well appear to be an overwhelming, even impossible, expectation to lay on any one person. The point to be made here, however, is not that preachers must know everything, but rather that there is no limit to the sources of knowledge and insight that a preacher can draw upon. There are many avenues which lead toward a deeper understanding of the human condition. Some will travel more easily down the avenue of the social sciences, others down the avenue of literature and the arts, others down the avenue of popular culture. What ultimately matters is not which avenue we take, but what we take with us as we travel.

[36] As long as we carry the Word of God with us, a word that we have allowed to touch on our own lives in prayer and reflection, and as long as we speak that word in language and images that are familiar to the dwellers of the particular avenue we are traveling, the Word of God will be preached, and the possibility of faith and conversion will be present.

The Limitations of the Preacher

[37] It may be good to close this section with a word of caution. While preachers, like other people, cannot be expected to know everything, they are easily tempted to give the impression that they do. As one perceptive critic put it, preachers in their pulpits are people who speak ten feet above contradiction. The Word of God which we are called to proclaim is a divinely inspired Word, and therefore an authoritative and unfailing Word. But we who are limited and fallible possess no guarantee that our understanding of this Word—or of the human situation—is without error and therefore relevant and binding.

[38] Preachers accept their limitations not by making the pulpit a sounding board for their personal doubts, anxieties or problems, but by offering people a Word which has spoken to their lives and inviting these people to think and ponder on that Word so that it might speak to their lives as well. A recent poster says it well: "Jesus came to take away our sins, not our minds." What preachers may need to witness to more than anything else is the conviction that authentic, mature faith demands the hard struggle of thinking and choosing. What the Word of God offers us is a way to interpret our human lives, a way to face the ambiguities and challenges of the human condition, not a pat answer to every problem and question that comes along.

[39] Some years ago a survey was taken among a group of parishioners. They were asked what they hoped to experience during a sermon. When the results were in, the answer was clear. What the majority wanted was simply to hear a person of faith speaking. Ultimately, that's what preaching is all about, not lofty theological speculation, not painstaking biblical exegesis, not oratorical flamboyance. The preacher is a person speaking to people about faith and life.

III. *The Homily*

[40] The Sunday Eucharist is a privileged point of encounter between a local Christian community and its priest. Within this

Eucharistic celebration the homily is a moment when this encounter can be especially intense and personal. We want now to look at the nature and function of this form of preaching, to relate it to the issues we have already raised in speaking of the assembly and the preacher, and finally to suggest a method for building and preaching the homily.

The Homily and Faith

[41] Like all preaching, the homily is directed to faith. As Paul writes, "But how shall they call on him in whom they have not believed? And how can they believe unless they have heard of him? And how can they hear unless there is someone to preach?" (Romans 10:14). Some preaching is directed to people who have not heard the Gospel and is meant to lead them to an initial acceptance of Jesus Christ as Savior. Other forms of preaching are directed to a deeper understanding of the faith or to its ethical implications.

[42] The homily is preaching of another kind. It may well include evangelization, catechesis, and exhortation, but its primary purpose is to be found in the fact that it is, in the words of the Second Vatican Council, "a part of the liturgy itself" (*Constitution on the Sacred Liturgy*, #52). The very meaning and function of the homily is determined by its relation to the liturgical action of which it is a part. It flows from the Scriptures which are read at that liturgical celebration, or, more broadly, from the Scriptures which undergird its prayers and actions, and it enables the congregation to participate in the celebration with faith.

[43] The fact that the homily is addressed to a congregation of believers who have gathered to worship indicates that its purpose is not conversion from radical unbelief to belief. A homily presupposes faith. Nor does the homily primarily concern itself with a systematic theological understanding of the faith. The liturgical gathering is not primarily an educational assembly. Rather the homily is preached in order that a community of believers who have gathered to celebrate the liturgy may do

so more deeply and more fully—more faithfully—and thus be formed for Christian witness in the world.[2]

Faith as Interpretation

[44] To say that preaching, the homily included, is directed to faith is another way of saying that preaching is involved in the task of interpretation. "Faith" can be defined as a way of seeing or interpreting the world. The way we interpret the world, in turn, determines the way we relate to it. For example, if we believe that a particular race or class of people are our enemies, we will relate to them with suspicion and hostility. A friendly gesture will be interpreted not as a genuine sign of good will but as a ruse to get us to lower our guard. On the other hand, if we believe that a group of people are our friends, we will tend to excuse even a hostile gesture with the explanation that there must have been some mistake: they didn't recognize us or we have misinterpreted their gesture. Our "faith" in the way things are has led us to live in the world in a way that corresponds to what we believe about it.

[45] The Christian interprets the world not as a hostile and evil place, but as a creation of a loving God who did not allow it to destroy itself, but sent his Son to rescue it. The Christian response to the world, then, is one of acceptance and affirmation—along with the recognition that it is still awaiting its full redemption.

[46] One of the most important, and most specifically human, ways in which faith is communicated to individuals and communities is through language. The way we speak about our world expresses the way we think about it and interpret it. One of the reasons we speak about our world at all is to share our vision of the world with others. The preacher is a Christian specially charged with sharing the Christian vision of the world as the creation of a loving God. Into this world human beings unleashed the powers of sin and death. These powers have been met, however, by God through his Son Jesus Christ, in whom he is at work not only to restore creation, but to transform it into a new heaven and a new earth.

Faith Leading to a Response

[47] When one hears and accepts this vision of the world, this way of interpreting reality, a response is required. That response can take many forms. Sometimes it will be appropriate to call people to repentance for the way they have helped to spread the destructive powers of sin in the world. At other times the preacher will invite the congregation to devote themselves to some specific action as a way of sharing in the redemptive and creative word of God. However, the response that is most general and appropriate "at all times and in every place" is the response of praise and thanksgiving (Eucharist).

[48] When we accept the good news that the ultimate root and source of our being is not some faceless Prime Mover, not a merciless judge, but a prodigally loving Father who calls us to share in his love and to spread it to others, we sense that it is indeed right to give him thanks and praise.

Although we have received this good news, believed in it, and sealed our belief in the sacrament of baptism, we need to rediscover the truth of it again and again in our lives. Our faith grows weak, we are deceived by appearances, overwhelmed by suffering, plagued by doubt, anguished by the dreadful silence of God. And yet we gather for Eucharist, awaiting a word that will rekindle the spark of faith and enable us to recognize once again the presence of a loving God in our lives. We come to break bread in the hope that we will be able to do so with hearts burning. We come expecting to hear a Word from the Lord that will again help us to see the meaning of our lives in such a way that we will be able to say, with faith and conviction, "It is right to give him thanks and praise."

[49] The preacher then has a formidable task: to speak from the Scriptures (those inspired documents of our tradition that hand down to us the way the first believers interpreted the world) to a gathered congregation in such a way that those assembled will be able to worship God in spirit and truth, and then go forth to love and serve the Lord. But while the task is formidable, it

is not impossible, especially if one goes about it with purpose and method.

The Homily and the Lectionary

[50] The homily is not so much on the Scriptures as *from* and *through* them. In the Roman Catholic tradition, the selection of texts to be read at the Eucharistic liturgy is normally not left to the preacher, but is determined ahead of time and presented in the form of a lectionary. The basic purpose of a lectionary is twofold: to ensure that the Scripture texts appropriate to a feast or season are read at that time, and to provide for a comprehensive reading of the Scriptures. Thus, we find in the lectionary two principles guiding the selection of texts: the thematic principle (readings chosen to correspond to the "theme" of a feast or season), and the *lectio continua* principle (readings taken in order from a book of the Bible which is being read over a given period of time).

[51] In the section of the lectionary entitled "Masses for Various Occasions," we find the thematic principle at work in a way that corresponds more closely to what some liturgical planners refer to as the theme of a liturgy: e.g., readings appropriate for Christian unity, or for peace and justice. Such thematic liturgies have their place, as the lectionary title indicates, on various or special occasions, rather than at the regular Sunday liturgy.[3]

[52] It is to these given texts that the preacher turns to prepare the homily for a community that will gather for the Sunday liturgy. Since the purpose of the homily is to enable the gathered congregation to celebrate the liturgy with faith, the preacher does not so much attempt to explain the Scriptures as to interpret the human situation through the Scriptures. In other words, the goal of the liturgical preacher is not to interpret a text of the Bible (as would be the case in teaching a Scripture class) as much as to draw on the texts of the Bible as they are presented in the lectionary to interpret peoples' lives. To be even more precise, the preacher's purpose will be to turn to these Scriptures to interpret

peoples' lives in such a way that they will be able to celebrate Eucharist—or be reconciled with God and one another, or be baptized into the Body of Christ, depending on the particular liturgy that is being celebrated.[4]

[53] To preach from the Scriptures in this way means that we have to "get behind them," as it were. We have to hear these texts as real words addressed to real people. Scholarly methods of interpreting Scripture can help us do this by putting us in touch with the life situations that originated these texts, or by making us more aware of the different ways language can function as a conveyer of meaning. But scholarly methods are not enough. As we emphasized in the second chapter, the preacher needs to listen to these texts meditatively and prayerfully.

[54] As preachers we go to the Scriptures saying, "What is the human situation to which these texts were originally addressed? To what human concerns and questions might these same texts have spoken through the Church's history? What is the human situation to which they can speak today? How can they help us to understand, to interpret our lives in such a way that we can turn to God with praise and thanksgiving?" Only when we approach the Scriptures in this way do they have any possibility of becoming a living word for us and for others.

[55] Such prayerful listening to the text demands time, not just the time of actual reading and praying and studying but, just as importantly, the time of standing back and letting the text dwell in our unconscious mind. This period of "incubation," as it is often called, is essential to all human creative effort. It is especially important for the homilist when reflecting upon texts which have become overly familiar, or which seem inappropriate for a given situation. With the use of a lectionary, the readings assigned for a particular day may seem to have little to say to a specific congregation at a specific time in its life. However, if the text and the actual human situation are allowed to interact with one another, a powerful interpretative word of faith will often emerge. But for this to happen we need to dwell with the text and allow it to dwell

with us. Only then will the text reveal new meaning to us, a new and fresh way of interpreting and speaking about our world.[5]

The Homily, the Congregation, and Homily Services

[56] If the homily must be faithful to the Scriptures for it to be the living Word of God, it must also be faithful to the congregation to whom this living Word of God is addressed. The homily will be effective in enabling a community to worship God with praise and thanksgiving only if individuals in that community recognize there a word that responds to the implicit or explicit questions of their lives.

[57] There are many ways in which priests get to know their congregations and allow themselves to be known by them: involvement with parish organizations, individual and family counseling, social contacts, visits to the sick and the bereaved, planning for weddings and baptisms, the sacrament of reconciliation, and, equally as important, simply being with people as a friend and member of the community. The preacher will be able to draw on all these contacts when he turns to the Scriptures to seek there a Word from the Lord for the lives of his people.

[58] This pastoral dimension of the homily is the principal reason why some homily services, especially those that do little more than provide ready-to-preach homilies, can actually be a hindrance to effective preaching. Since the homily is integrally related to the liturgy, and since liturgy presupposes a community that gathers to celebrate it, the homily is by definition related to a community. Homily services can be helpful in the interpretation of scriptural texts (though generally not as much as some basic exegetical resources) and give some ideas on how these texts can be related to contemporary human concerns. But they cannot provide individual preachers with specific indications of how these texts can be heard by the particular congregations to whom they will preach.

[59] Homily services can provide valuable assistance to the preacher when they are concerned to relate the interpretation of

the lectionary texts to the liturgical season in which they appear, and when they are attentive to the *lectio continua* principle of the lectionary. They may also be helpful in suggesting some possibilities for the development of a homily, or in providing suitable examples and illustrations. The primary help that a good homily service will offer is to make available to the preacher recent exegetical work on the specific texts that appear in the lectionary and to indicate some ways in which this biblical word can be heard in the present as God's Word to his people. They can never replace the homilist's own prayer, study, and work.

The Homily and the Liturgy of the Eucharist

[60] A homily is not a talk given on the occasion of a liturgical celebration. It is "a part of the liturgy itself." In the Eucharistic celebration the homily points to the presence of God in people's lives and then leads a congregation into the Eucharist, providing, as it were, the motive for celebrating the Eucharist in this time and place.[6]

[61] This integral relation of the homily to the liturgy of the Eucharist which follows the liturgy of the word has implications for the way in which the homily is composed and delivered. In the first place, the homily should flow quite naturally out of the readings and into the liturgical action that follows. To set the homily apart by beginning or ending it with a sign of the cross[7], or by delivering it in a style that is totally different from the style used in the rest of the liturgy, might only reinforce the impression that the homily is simply a talk given on the occasion of a liturgical gathering, one that could just as well be given at another time and in another context.

[62] Although the preaching of the homily properly belongs to the presiding minister of the Eucharistic celebration, there may occasionally be times when it is fitting for someone else, priest or deacon, to preach. On these occasions the integral relation of the homily to the rest of the liturgy will be safeguarded if the preacher is present and actively involved in the whole of the li-

turgical celebration. The practice of having a preacher slip in to read the Gospel and preach the homily, and then slip out again, does not do justice to the liturgical integrity of the homily.

Homiletic Style

[63] As regards the structure and style of the homily, we can take a lead from the use of the Greek word *homileo* in the New Testament.[8] While the etymology of the word suggests communicating with a crowd, its actual use in the New Testament implies a more personal and conversational form of address than that used by the classical Greek orator. The word is employed in reference to the conversation the two disciples engaged in on their way to Emmaus (Luke 24:14) and of the conversation Antonius Felix, Procurator of Judea, had with Paul when the latter was held prisoner in Caesarea (Acts 24:26). The New Testament usage suggests that a homily should sound more like a personal conversation, albeit a conversation on matters of utmost importance, than like a speech or a classroom lecture. What we should strive for is a style that is purposeful and personal, avoiding whatever sounds casual and chatty on the one extreme or impersonal and detached on the other.

[64] One of the ways we can move toward a more personal style of address in our homilies is by the way we structure them. Many homilies seem to fall into the same three-part pattern: "In today's readings . . . This reminds us . . . Therefore let us . . ." The very structure of such homilies gives the impression that the preacher's principal purpose is to interpret scriptural texts rather than communicate with real people, and that he interprets these texts primarily to extract ethical demands to impose on a congregation. Such preachers may offer good advice, but they are rarely heard as preachers of good news, and this very fact tends to distance them from their listeners.

[65] Another way of structuring the homily, and one that is more in keeping with its function of enabling people to celebrate the liturgy with deepened faith, is to begin with a description of a

contemporary human situation which is evoked by the scriptural texts, rather than with an interpretation or reiteration of the text. After the human situation has been addressed, the homilist can turn to the Scriptures to interpret this situation, showing how the God described therein is also present and active in our lives today. The conclusion of the homily can then be an invitation to praise this God who wills to be lovingly and powerfully present in the lives of his people.[9]

[66] The point of the preceding paragraph is not to substitute a new straight jacket for an old one. There is no one correct form for the homily. On occasion it may be a dramatic and engaging story, on another a well-reasoned exposition of a biblical theme showing its relevance to the contemporary situation, or the liturgical day, feast or season. It might also take the form of a dialogue between two preachers or involve the approved local use of visual or audio media. Ideally, the form and style will be determined by the form and style of the Scriptures from which it flows, by the character of the liturgy of which it is a part, and by the composition and expectations of the congregation to which it is addressed, and not exclusively by the preference of the preacher.

[67] Whatever its form, the function of the Eucharistic homily is to enable people to lift up their hearts, to praise and thank the Lord for his presence in their lives. It will do this more effectively if the language it uses is specific, graphic, and imaginative. The more we can turn to the picture language of the poet and the storyteller, the more we will be able to preach in a way that invites people to respond from the heart as well as from the mind.

The Limits and Possibilities of Liturgical Preaching

[68] But isn't all this too limited a view of preaching? Does it really respond to the needs of the people? Doesn't regular Sunday preaching have to take into account the ignorance of the Scriptures on the part of large numbers of Catholics, even those who participate regularly in the Sunday Eucharist, and deal

in some systematic way with the fundamentals of the faith? Is there not a crying need for regular and sustained teaching about the moral imperatives that flow from an acceptance of the Good News? What about all those times when people's lives are shattered, when they simply are psychologically incapable of offering God praise and thanks, when it seems they have nothing to be thankful for? How do we speak to all the people in our congregations who have yet to hear the basic Gospel message calling them to faith and conversation, or who may even need a form of preaching that heightens their sensitivity to basic human realities and in this way readies them for the hearing of the Gospel?

[69] In the last analysis the only proper response to these questions is a pastoral one. Priests will have to decide what form of preaching is most suitable for a particular congregation at a particular time. We would simply like to make two points here. First of all, social science research contends that the oral presentation of a single person is not a particularly effective way to impart new information or to bring about a change in attitude or behavior. It is, however, well suited to make explicit or to reinforce attitudes or knowledge previously held. The homily, therefore, which normally is an oral presentation by a single person, will be less effective as a means of instruction and/or exhortation than of interpretation—that is, as a means of enabling people to recognize the implications, in liturgy and in life, of the faith that is already theirs.

[70] The second point to be made is that the liturgical homily, which draws on the Scriptures to interpret peoples' lives in such a way that they can recognize the saving presence of God and turn to him with praise and thanksgiving, does not exclude doctrinal instruction and moral exhortation. Such instruction and exhortation, however, are here situated in a broader context, namely, in the recognition of God's active presence in the lives of the people and the praise and thanksgiving that this response elicits.[10]

[71] It may very well be that what God is doing in the life of a congregation at some particular moment is asking them to change in a way that is demanding and disorienting. The homily can be one way of helping to bring about that change, and it can still lead to a response of praise and thanksgiving by showing that our former way of life, comfortable as it may have been, was a way that led to death, while the new way, with all of its demands and difficulties, is a way that leads to life.

[72] But even though the liturgical homily can incorporate instruction and exhortation, it will not be able to carry the whole weight of the Church's preaching. There will still need to be special times and occasions for preaching that addresses human values in such a way as to dispose the hearers to be open to the Gospel of Jesus Christ, preaching intended to bring the hearers to an inner conversion of heart, and preaching intended to instruct the faithful in matters of doctrine or morality. These three kinds of preaching—sometimes referred to as pre-evangelization, evangelization, and catechesis—can be found today in evangelistic gatherings, the adult catechumenate, youth ministry programs, spiritual renewal programs, Bible study groups and many forms of religious education.

[73] The homily can complement all these forms of preaching by attending more specifically to what it is to accomplish. Such would be to show how and where the mystery of our faith, focused upon by that day's Scripture readings, is occurring in our lives. This would bring the hearers to a more explicit and deepened faith, to an expression of that faith in the liturgical celebration and, following the celebration, in their life and work.

[74] But is it really possible to create this readiness for praise and thanksgiving in congregations as large and diverse as those in which many of us minister? In these congregations some people will be feeling a sense of loss because of a recent bereavement; some facing marital difficulties; some having problems adjusting emotionally to school, job, home or community; some struggling with a deep sense of guilt stemming from their inability to deal

maturely with their sexuality, or because of their addiction to drugs or alcohol. Others in our congregations will be struggling with the relevance of the Gospel to oppressive economic structures, to world peace, or to the many forms of discrimination in our society. Is it really possible to say to these people, "Look at the way in which God is present in your lives and turn to him with praise and thanksgiving?"

[75] Obviously, it will not always be easy to do this. And we will never be able to do it, at least not with any honesty and integrity, if we have not recognized the active presence of God in our own lives, as broken and shattered as they may be, and out of that brokenness affirm that it is still good to praise him and even to give him thanks. We need to remember in situations like this that our celebration of the Eucharist is done in memory of Jesus Christ who, *on the night before he died*, turned to God and praised and thanked him out of the very depths of his distress. Praise and thanksgiving, therefore, do not automatically imply the presence of euphoria.

[76] We can and must praise God even when we do not feel like it, for praise and thanksgiving are rooted in and grow out of faith, not feeling, a faith which interprets this world by saying that in spite of appearances often to the contrary, our God is a loving God. It is for this reason that even at the time of death, we celebrate a Eucharist, because we believe that for his faithful ones life is changed, not, as appearances would seem to indicate, taken away.

[77] The challenge to preachers then is to reflect on human life with the aid of the Word of God and to show by their preaching, as by their lives, that in every place and at every time it is indeed right to praise and thank the Lord.

IV. Homiletic Method

[78] Every art is based on a theory and a method, and preaching is no exception. Some artists, it is true, work solely from

inspiration. They do not know why or how they do what they do. Consequently, they are incapable of passing their insight on to others. But they have a method nonetheless, and if their work is lasting, their method will sooner or later be uncovered by interpreters and critics of their work.

[79] Artists who are conscious of their method are in a much more advantageous position than those who are not. They are able to channel and direct their work more easily, can work more efficiently within time constraints, and can adapt their method to changed circumstances and demands. They know what they are doing and how they go about doing it, and they can pass this information on to others who might like to learn from them.

[80] Ultimately, individual preachers will have to develop their own method for moving from the Scriptures to the homily, learning from their own successes and failures, as well as from other preachers through whose words they have heard the Word of God. The description of a method for building the homily that follows is not intended as—nor could it possibly be—a foolproof system for producing outstanding homilies week after week. Rather it provides a model that includes the major components of the creative process (data gathering, incubation, insight, communication) and does so within the framework of a week.

[81] This method also respects the understanding of the homily that is central to this document: a scriptural interpretation of human existence which enables a community to recognize God's active presence, to respond to that presence in faith through liturgical word and gesture, and beyond the liturgical assembly, through a life lived in conformity with the Gospel.

[82] The most important feature of any method is precisely that it be methodical, that is, orderly and regular. In the preparation of the homily, as in other creative endeavors, the total amount of time we spend preparing may be less important than our observance of a regular pattern of activity spread out over a certain period of time. Doing the same thing each day for the same amount of time is often a condition for success, whether

this be in study, in prayer, in writing, or in artistic achievement. A regular daily pattern of activity for the preparation of the Sunday homily is likewise often the key factor in effective preaching over the long term.

[83] Each of us called to the regular ministry of preaching needs to determine just what part of each day of the week is going to be devoted to the preparation of the Sunday homily. The time we spend each day need not be lengthy, but it needs to be determined ahead of time and be held sacred. Schedules, of course, are always to be adjusted for emergencies, but unless we determine in advance that a particular time is going to be used for a particular purpose, and stick to it, it is all too easy to have our entire day filled with appointments and meetings which we felt we could not turn down or postpone because "we had nothing special planned."

[84] One final preliminary remark. The method that follows describes a process that extends over a week's time. Some form of "remote preparation" is also in order. Such preparation could take the form of reading a recent work on the theology of the particular Synoptic Gospel that will be the "Gospel of the Year" or spending some time planning a unified sequence of homilies for a particular liturgical season.

[85] One of the reasons our preaching is less effective than it could be is that we have not taken seriously enough the *lectio continua* principle of our lectionary. We preach each Sunday's homily as if it had no connection with what preceded or what will follow. It should be possible, and indeed it would emphasize a sense of continuity and identity in the congregation, if from time to time our homilies would end on a "to be continued" note.

Reading, Listening, Praying

[86] The preparation for a Sunday homily should begin early in the week whenever possible, even on Sunday evening. The first step is to read and reread the texts for the liturgy. Frequently the texts will be familiar, so it is important for us to do everything

we can to make this reading as fresh as possible. Read the texts aloud; read them in several versions; if we read and understand Greek or Hebrew, we might try to read them in the original. Even if our knowledge of these languages is minimal, we may find ourselves becoming aware of nuances and connections that can easily be missed if we rely entirely on translations.

[87] At this point in the preparation process it is helpful, indeed almost essential, to read the texts in context—that is, to read them from the Bible rather than from the lectionary only. In reading and rereading the texts, continue to read all four of them (Gospel, Old Testament, Psalm, New Testament), even if a decision has been made about which text will become the focus of the homily. It is not necessary for a homily to tie together all the readings. Indeed, for the Sundays throughout the year, when the New Testament lesson is chosen without reference to the Old Testament or the Gospel, attempts to impose some kind of thematic unity can be quite artificial. Nonetheless, the reading of the texts side by side, even if they are unrelated to one another, can often prompt new and rich insights into the "now" meaning of the Scriptures.

[88] Read the texts with pen in hand, jotting down any and all ideas. Keep in mind that what we are listening for is a Word from the Lord, a Word which can be heard as good news. We will be all the more disposed to hear and receive such a word if our reading is a prayerful, attentive listening to the text of the Scriptures. Try to read the text without asking "What does it mean?" Approach it humbly, dwell with it, and let it speak for itself.

Study and Further Reflection

[89] One of the major temptations of students when they are assigned a paper is immediately to run to the "experts." The same temptation afflicts preachers. All too often our preparation for a homily consists of looking up the lessons, reading them over quickly, and then turning to a commentary or a homily service to find out what they mean and what we might be able

to say about them. By so doing we block out the possibility of letting these texts speak to us and to the concerns we share with a congregation.

[90] Another danger in going to the commentaries too early is that we program ourselves for preaching which, in content and style, is academic rather than existential. We look for information about the texts that we can pass on to our hearers. We think of the text as a container of a hidden meaning that we have to discover and pry loose with the appropriate tools, rather than as a word spoken directly to us by the Lord. This approach to the text leads to preaching that is a word about something rather than a word, God's Word, to someone.

[91] The process of personal reflection and interpretation, therefore, should go on for a couple of days without the aid of commentaries. We are our own interpreters first of all, and then when we do turn to the professional exegetes, we do so for the purpose of checking out the accuracy of our own interpretation. We will frequently receive new insights and ideas from the professionals, and these will be helpful to us. If we have allowed the texts to speak to us directly, we will be much better prepared to speak a word that is expressive of our own faith and in touch with the concerns of our people. We will also be able to better recognize and use the insights the professional exegetes give us.

Letting Go

[92] Sometime in the middle of the preparation process we should allow ourselves to step back from the work we are doing and give free reign to the subconscious processes of our minds. At times we will find that our preparation has brought us to a roadblock. A passage may make no sense to us. It may even scandalize us. We may want to ignore it, but it will not go away. The more we wrestle with it, the more troublesome it becomes. The words of Jesus about love for enemies fly in the face of our natural inclination for retribution; his words about selling possessions and giving them to the poor contradict our instinctive

sense of the necessity for prudent stewardship. Paul's teaching that sin and death entered the world through one man seems to contradict everything we hold about individual, personal freedom and responsibility. We sense a real tension between the Word of God and the human situation.

[93] When this happens we have one of the best signs that we are on to something vital. The Word of God may in fact be challenging our faith, calling us to conversion, to a new vision of the world. This period can be a difficult one, for we can feel that we are being asked to give up a way of looking at and dealing with the world which has served us well and with which we have grown comfortable. At a time like this we need to let go in order to allow the Holy Spirit to work within us and lead us to a deeper and richer faith.

Drafting

[94] A time for writing should be scheduled at least two days before the preaching of the homily in order to provide ample time for alterations. Knowing that there will be opportunity to rework the homily will do much to save us from writer's block. At this stage we need not be concerned with matters of style, or even with making sure that the homily is tightly reasoned and well constructed. The point is simply to begin getting ideas down on paper so that we will have something to work with.

[95] It is quite possible that we will come to this stage of preparation still not having any idea—any new and fresh idea, that is—of what we are going to say. We may simply feel empty and without inspiration. Begin writing anyway, for the very act of writing often unleashes a flow of ideas that will be new, fresh, and exciting. It is often at this point of initial writing that the difficult text suddenly opens up its meaning and provides a new, a richer understanding of how God is present in our lives. At this point, too, the two readings which had seemed so totally unrelated may suddenly come together and illuminate one another. When something like this happens (sometimes referred

to as the moment of insight, or the "aha" experience), we may well have the central idea for our homily.

[96] So, at this point, simply write. Jot down words, phrases, unrelated sentences. Think of sketching the homily, or of working on an outline, rather than writing out a text. In fact, it is better not to put the ideas in too fixed a form at this point, for we may find that it then becomes difficult to alter them. Don't stop to think of the best way to say something; don't go back and cross out words and phrases because they don't sound right. There is time for that later. Let the pen or the typewriter simply go, even though we are sure that we will not use anything we are putting down on paper. The very act of writing is a way of calling to the surface the ideas and the words that will in fact be the stuff of which our homilies are made.

Revising

[97] The revising stage is one of the most important and the one that is too easily omitted for lack of time. To revise is frequently to cut: the good but extraneous material that surfaced in the jotting down stage of preparation; the technical theological terms and jargony "in" words that creep into our vocabularies; the use of the non-specific "this" or "it" at the beginning of sentences; the moralistic "therefore let us" or "we should" which we so easily resort to in winding up the homily; the references to "he" and "men" when the words are meant to include everyone; the vague generalities that can be replaced with specific incidents or examples.

[98] The time for revising is also the time to arrange the material in the order best suited to gain, and hold, people's attention and to invite them to a response of faith in God's Word. In the sketching stage a story may have occurred to us which exemplified perfectly the human situation being addressed by the Word of God. Bring that story up front. Use it as the opening so that people are able to identify with the situation right from the beginning. Beginning the homily with "in today's Gospel

. . ." or words to that effect, risks losing the attention of the congregation right at the beginning for they will not have been given any indication of why they should be interested in what was said in today's Gospel.

[99] The time of revising is also the time to make sure that the homily does in fact have a central, unifying idea, and that this idea is clearly stated and repeated throughout the homily. We need not repeat the idea in the same words all the time, but we need to come back to it several times. People will inevitably drift in and out, no matter how good the preacher is. The restatement of the central idea is a way of inviting people back into the homily again if they happen to have been distracted from what we were saying.

[100] Finally, the time for revising is the time to make sure that the homily is fashioned not simply as a freestanding talk, but as an integral part of the liturgical action. Does the conclusion in any way lead people into the liturgy that follows? Have we spoken the Word of God in such a way that God has become more present in people's lives and they are enabled to be drawn more fully into the act of worship for which they have gathered? Remember that a homily is not a talk given on the occasion of a liturgical celebration, but an integral part of the liturgy. Just as a homily flows out of the Scriptures of the liturgy of the Word, so it should flow into the prayers and actions of the liturgy of the Eucharist which follows.

Practicing

[101] After revising the homily, practice it. Repeat it several times to become familiar with what has to be said and how to say it. Practice it aloud and ask if that is really "me" speaking. Does it sound natural, or have I introduced words and phrases that sounded good when I jotted them down but are not suited to oral communication? It may be helpful to preach the homily to a friend or co-worker or to use an audio/video tape recorder. Can I say to that person without embarrassment what I intend to

say to the congregation? Do I really believe what I am saying, or have I hidden behind some conventional expression of piety or theology that I would probably not use in any other situation?

Preaching

[102] Our emphasis on the importance of writing in the preparation of a homily does not in any way imply that homilies should normally be read. Writing is a means to arrive at good organization, clarity of expression, and concreteness. Whether or not we actually take a manuscript to the pulpit with us will depend on a number of things: the nature of the gathering (very formal or more informal); how familiar we are with our own material; how apprehensive we feel about forgetting something essential.

[103] Sometimes we know what we are going to say so well, and are so enthused about it that a manuscript would only get in the way or distract us. On the other hand, there may be times when we are sure that our message will be clearer and more forceful if we have the text with us. As long as we have something to say, as long as we are saying it, and as long as we establish and maintain rapport with the congregation, we may be able to preach quite effectively from a text.

[104] In general, it is much better to speak from notes or an outline—or without any written aids at all, for such a way of preaching enables us to enter more fully into direct, personal contact with a congregation. If we feel we must take the text with us, be familiar enough with the material so that instead of reading it, we can simply have it present as an aid to our memory.

[105] In preaching, as in all forms of communication, remember that it is the whole person who communicates. Facial expression, the tone of voice, the posture of the body are all powerful factors in determining whether a congregation will be receptive to what we have to say. If, as we preach, we remember that in carrying out this ministry we are showing our love, and God's, for the people, we will more easily avoid a delivery that sounds affected ("churchy") or impersonal.

The Homily Preparation Group

[106] An effective way for preachers to be sure that they are addressing some of the real concerns of the congregation in the homily is to involve members of that congregation in a homily preparation group. One way to begin such a group is for the preachers to invite four or five people they trust and can work with easily to join them for an hour at the beginning of the week. In a parish setting it is advisable to have one of the members drop out after four weeks and invite someone else to take his or her place. Similarly, a second will drop out after the fifth week, so that after eight weeks or so they will be working with a new group of people.

[107] A homily preparation group can also be formed by gathering the priests in the rectory, the parish staff, priests from the area, priest and ministers, or a priests' support group. The presence of members of the congregation in a group is especially helpful in raising issues that are of concern to them and which the homily may be able to address. Groups that involve only clergy or parish staff members can also be a rich source of insight into the ways in which the Scriptures point to the continuing presence of God in human history.

[108] After the group has gathered and spent a few minutes quieting down, the following steps can be followed:

1. Read the passages (15 minutes). Begin with the Gospel, then the Old Testament, Psalm, and New Testament. As one of the participants reads the passages slowly, the others listen and jot down images, words or phrases that strike them.

2. Share the words (10 minutes). This is not a time for discussion but simply an opportunity for each person to share the words or phrases which resonated and fired the imagination. As this sharing is going on, the homilist may pick up some recurring words and phrases. He may be surprised to hear what parts of the Scriptures are being highlighted. These responses are already a sign of the concerns, questions and interests that are present in the lives of the congregation.

3. Exegete the texts (10 minutes). One of the members of the group presents a short exegesis of the texts. The task is not to bring to the discussion everything that could be said, but to make a special effort to determine what concrete human concerns the author was addressing when the text was written. What questions were there to which these words were at least a partial answer? When dealing with the Gospel passage, one way to answer this question is to show how other evangelists treated the same materials.

4. Share the good news (10 minutes). What good news did the first listeners hear in these accounts? What good news does the group hear? Where is God's promise, power and influence in our personal story present in the readings?

5. Share the challenge these words offer us (10 minutes). What is the doubt, the sin, the pain, the fracturing in our own lives which the passage touches? To what form of conversion do these words call us? In responding to these questions, the group may resort to generalities. By gentle persuasion and personal example the homilist can encourage the group to speak personally and with examples.

6. Explore the consequences (5 minutes). What difference can the good news make in my life? What happens if the scriptural good news is applied to contemporary bad news? Can my life be changed? Can the world be transformed if people believe in the good news and begin acting according to it? These are questions to which final answers cannot be given. They demand prayer and reflection.

7. Give thanks and praise (5 minutes). Conclude with a brief prayer of thanksgiving for God's saving Word.

Working with a homily preparation group will help to ensure two things: that the homilist hears the proclamation of the good news in the Sunday Scripture readings as it is heard by the people in the congregation; and secondly, that the preacher is able to point in concrete and specific ways to the difference that the hearing of this good news can make in the lives of those who hear it. When the preacher spends time with the congregation, struggling with how the Word touches real life, the possibility of this homily striking a listener as "talking to me" increases. The

Word of God then achieves that for which it was sent. Preacher and listener, responding together, are nourished by the Word of God and drawn to praise the God who has again given a sign of his presence and power.

The Non-negotiables of Homily Preparation

[109] As we mentioned at the beginning of this chapter, there is no one way to prepare a homily, nor does a particular method work the same way all the time for the same person. But no matter what the method, there are certain elements in the preparation of the homily which cannot be omitted if our preaching over the long term is going to be scripturally sound and pastorally relevant. We may be able to "wing it" on occasion, but to try to sustain a weekly ministry of preaching with little more than a glance at the lectionary and the quick consultation of a homily service is to attempt the impossible.

[110] Effective preaching—that is, preaching that enables people to hear the Word of God as good news for their lives and to respond accordingly—requires time and serious work. Unless we are willing to accept the drudgery that is a part of preaching, as it is of all creative work, we will not know the joy of having the Scriptures come alive for us, nor the profoundly satisfying experience of sharing that discovery with others.

[111] To conclude this chapter on homiletic method we would point to what we consider to be the non-negotiable elements of effective preaching:

1. Time. The amount of time will vary from preacher to preacher. However, the importance of the ministry of preaching demands that a significant amount of time be devoted to the homily each week, and ideally, that this time be spread out over the entire week.

2. Prayer. All preaching flows from faith to faith. It is only through prayer that faith is nourished.

3. Study. Without continuing study, stagnation sets in and preaching becomes insipid. Preachers have a professional responsibility to continue their education in the areas of Scripture, theology, and related disciplines. They might well make a book on preaching part of their regular reading program.

4. Organization. Much preaching suffers from lack of direction and the absence of a central, controlling idea. The writing and revising of homilies helps to ensure that there is a point to what we preach.

5. Concreteness. Another common fault of preachers is their tendency to speak in vague generalities or to use technical theological language. Once again, writing and revising helps to ensure that homilies are concrete and specific.

6. Evaluation. In public discourse we easily fall back on familiar ideas and set patterns of speech. More often than not, we are unaware of such tendencies and need the feedback of others to alert us to them.

Epilogue: The Power Of The Word

[112] The pulpit of St. Stephen's Cathedral in Vienna displays an elaborate handrail in which are carved a detailed series of ugly, mythical creatures. The open mouths and oversized snouts of the beasts are there to remind the preacher of his inadequacies as he ascends the stairs. At the very top of the handrail, carved into the pillar that separates the stairs from the open, circular pulpit, stands a dog, jaws open, barking down at the ominous figures. The hellish beasts are not to enter the sacred place. The preacher has been enjoined to leave his sinful self behind as he prepares to speak God's Word.

[113] The medieval artisan has captured in stone the inner tension of all of us who dare to preach. We are aware that the words we speak are human words, formed through reflection both on the Scriptures and on our personal experience of the needs of our community. Looking into the faces of the people who sit before us, we see those who are holier, more intelligent, and more creative. And yet they wait for us to speak, to preach, to proclaim and witness to the presence of God among us. Our theology tells us

that the words we speak are also God's Word. "What we utter is God's wisdom, a mysterious, a hidden wisdom" (1 Cor 2:7).

[114] We dare to utter that sacred Word because we once heard the voice of Mystery who spoke to Isaiah: "Whom shall I send? Who will go for us?" And we answered with Isaiah, "Here I am; send me" (Is 6:8). With Jeremiah we trust that the Lord will place his words in our mouths, despite our youth or age, our ignorance and our inadequacies (Jer 1:6–9). Even when we fall on our faces, the promise of Ezechiel is there, that a voice will speak to us and a spirit enter into us and set us again on our feet (Ezek 2:1–3). We believe that the Word we speak is the Word God intends to have an effect upon the world in which we live.

> For just as from the heavens the rain and snow come
> And do not return there till they have watered the earth, making it fertile and fruitful,
> Giving seed to him who sows and bread to him who eats,
> So shall my word be that goes forth from my mouth;
> It shall not return to me void, but shall do my will, achieving the end for which I sent it. (Is 55:10–11)

[115] We too stand in sacred space, aware of our personal inadequacy, yet willing to share how the scriptural story has become integrated into our thoughts and actions while we walked among those who turn their faces toward us. The words we speak are human words describing how God's action has become apparent to us this week. Is it any wonder then that excitement and tension fill us in the moments before we preach? With a final deep breath may we also breathe in the Spirit of God who will animate our human words with divine power.

Appendix

[116] This document on preaching has dealt mainly with what the individual preacher can do to improve the quality of the Sunday homily. In conclusion, we offer some recommendations

for steps that can be taken on the national, diocesan, and parish levels to foster more effective preaching.

National

[117] 1. A doctoral program in homiletics to prepare teachers of preaching should be established with diocesan support, perhaps at the Catholic University of America.

2. Seminaries, especially at the theologate level, are urged to emphasize preaching as a priority (cf. *Program of Priestly Formation*, 3rd Edition, Chapter III, Art. 2, Homiletics).

Diocesan

[118] 1. Programs to improve preaching skills should be established at the diocesan or regional level.

2. Programs for the study and deeper understanding of Scripture and preaching theology should also be established.

3. A Center for Preaching Resources should be founded in each diocese by the diocesan office for worship or continuing education, or by the seminary.

4. The Bishop(s) of the diocese should model the nature and purpose of the homily in preaching. They should not accept more preaching engagements per day than allow for preparation.

5. Criteria for the granting of faculties to preach should be clearly formulated and followed.

6. Continuing development of good preaching should be supported by the diocese through the granting of time and funding.

Parish

[119] 1. A resource center should be established within each parish to assist preachers and lectors in fulfilling their ministry.

2. Groups to help preachers prepare and evaluate their homilies should be formed.

3. When there are several preachers in a parish, their preparation for preaching should be coordinated.

4. Readers should be trained in the effective proclamation of Scripture and provided opportunities to grow in their understanding of it.

5. Job descriptions for priests should be evaluated in order to highlight the importance and provide adequate time for preparation of the ministry of preaching.

6. Some record should be kept of the themes of each Sunday's homily in order to bring the parish community into contact with the major facets of our faith each year, and to avoid undue emphasis on one truth at the expense of others.

* * *

[120] At all levels, national, diocesan and parish, bishops and priests are urged to invite religious and laity to read this document so as to assist, encourage and support priests in efforts toward a renewal of preaching in the church.

Endnotes

1. The material on "audience analysis" is voluminous. Access to the most up-to-date studies can be found by consulting the bibliographies of recent books on speech communication. Such materials frequently describe various methods for determining with some accuracy the interest and abilities of an audience.

2. While the homily is not the same as catechetical instruction, as Pope Paul VI makes clear in his apostolic exhortation *Evangelii nuntiandi* (nos. 43 and 44), the homily can certainly be a means of catechesis for Christian communities. The homilist who preaches from the Scriptures as these are arranged in the lectionary over a three-year cycle of Sundays and feasts will certainly deal with all the major truths of the faith. It will still be necessary, however, to provide educational opportunities in and through which the faithful can reflect more deeply on the meaning of these truths and on their concrete contemporary implications for Christian life. In the early church such a systematic presentation of the truths of the faith was given to the newly baptized in the post-baptismal preaching known as mystagogy.

3. A fuller description of the principles guiding the choice of readings can be found in the introduction to the lectionary. These principles

should be familiar to all preachers, for a knowledge of how and why passages of Scripture are assigned to certain times and feasts provides an important key to the liturgical interpretation of those readings in preaching.

4. Cf. *Lectionary for Mass*. English translation of the Second *Editio-Typica* (1981) #24 prepared by International Commission on English in the Liturgy.

5. Ibid. #8–10.

6. Ibid. #24.

7. With regard to the sign of the cross before and after the homily, the Congregation for the Sacraments and Divine Worship gave the following official *responsum* in 1973:

> Query: Is it advisable to invite the faithful to bless themselves before or after the homily, to address a salutation to them, for example, "Praised be Jesus Christ"? Reply: It all depends on lawful local custom. But generally speaking it is inadvisable to continue such customs because they have their origin in preaching *outside* Mass. The homily is *part* of the liturgy; the people have already blessed themselves and received the greeting at the beginning of Mass. It is better, then, not to have a repetition before or after the homily. Source: *Notitiae* 29 (1973) 178.

8. *Keryssein*, "To proclaim," is the word most frequently used for preaching in the New Testament. The word "presupposes that the preachers are heralds who announce simply that which they are commissioned to announce, not in their own name, but by the authority of the one who sends them" (John L. McKenzie, *Dictionary of the Bible*, p. 689). Although the practice of first-century Jewish synagogues may have included explanations and applications of the Scriptures as part of the regular service, the New Testament itself does not use a specific technical word to describe the kind of preaching we refer to as a "homily," that is, the exposition of a text of scripture which takes place in and as a part of a liturgical celebration. The word *homileo* does appear in the New Testament, and its usage there can provide a way to understand a homiletic approach to preaching as distinguished from preaching addressed to unbelievers (*kerygma*).

9. The continuing ability of Scripture texts to speak to situations that are temporally and culturally distinct from those to which they were originally addressed is one way in which the canonicity of the Scriptures continues to be affirmed by the church. The canon is, in fact, composed

of those writings which the church considers too important to forget because they address issues which are present in every generation, albeit in different garb and guises.

10. In the Apostolic Exhortation, *On Catechesis in Our Time*, 1979, #48, Pope John Paul II observes, "Respecting the specific nature and proper cadence of this setting [i.e., liturgy, especially the Eucharistic assembly], the homily takes up again the journey of faith put forward by catechesis and brings it to its natural fulfillment. At the same time it encourages the Lord's disciples to begin anew each day their spiritual journey in truth, adoration and thanksgiving. Accordingly, one can say that catechetical teaching, too, finds its source and fulfillment in the Eucharist, within the whole circle of the liturgical year.

"Preaching, centered upon the Bible texts, must then in its own way make it possible to familiarize the faithful with the whole of the mysteries of the faith and the norms of Christian living . . . ." Cf. also: *Sharing the Light of Faith*, An Official Commentary on the National Catechetical Directory for Catholics of the United States, 1981, p. 54, Office of Publishing Services, USCC, Washington, D.C.

Appendix B

Fulfilled in Your Hearing: A Narrative History

Trish Sullivan Vanni

The Second Vatican Ecumenical Council (1962–65) in its call for a renewed liturgy, which it recognized as the "source and summit of the Christian life" (*Dogmatic Constitution on the Church*, 11), sought to facilitate the "full, conscious, and active participation" of the faithful (*Constitution on the Sacred Liturgy*; hereafter, *CSL*, 14). While changes such as the use of the vernacular, having the priest face the people, and giving communion under both species were most noticeable, other, subtler changes had an equal, if not greater, impact on the worship of the church. Not least of these was the enhanced role assigned to the homily in the Mass, now "strongly recommended since it forms part of the liturgy itself" (*CSL*, 52). Now with a clear focus on the Scriptures and liturgical texts of the day, the homily had been declared integral to the liturgy (*CSL*, 35, 2) and a primary duty of the priest (*Decree on the Ministry and Life of Priests*, 4).

Throughout the 1970s, the Roman Catholic Church in the United States struggled to integrate this renewed understanding of the liturgical homily. Ultimately, the United States Conference of Catholic Bishops authorized and approved *Fulfilled in Your Hearing: The Homily in the Sunday Assembly*, a landmark document on the nature and purpose of the homily, along with a method for homily development. Since it was published in 1982, this innovative document has helped shape how the American church understands the art and craft of preaching. The story of the forces that produced it, the documents that shaped it, and the unique contributors who wrote it, is a fascinating example of how successfully to integrate the teaching of a council into the life of the local church.

The Council's Impact on Preaching

With Vatican II's *CSL* asserting that the homily was to be recommended as part of the liturgy itself (52), expectations grew that preaching would be more explicitly rooted in biblical and liturgical sources and embrace a historical-critical exegesis of texts. Prior to the 1960s, it was commonplace for preaching to focus exclusively on moral exhortation or catechetical teaching, and it was not unusual for Sunday preaching to be a sermon sent out by the bishop on some aspect of the Our Father, the Creed, or the Christian moral life.

The scriptural focus of the homily in *CSL* was further supported by the publication of the Latin edition of the Roman Lectionary in 1969. The new lectionary included a far greater proportion of the Bible's content than the *Roman Missal*, which had gone largely unrevised since Trent. The new three-year cycle of biblical readings for Sundays and the two-year cycle for weekdays fulfilled the council's vision that "the treasures of the bible are to be opened up more lavishly, so that a richer fare may be provided for the faithful at the table of God's word" (*CSL*, 51). The publication of lectionary aids and preaching helps, along with new commentaries from biblical scholars, supported the council's vision that preaching be focused on the scriptural and liturgical texts of the day.

Implementing Change

After Vatican II, achieving "noble simplicity" became a guideline for revising liturgical rites, including the Roman Missal, the

Roman Pontifical, the Ceremonial of Bishops, and the Liturgy of the Hours. But the task of implementing liturgical changes—including the renewal of homiletic method—was entrusted to the episcopal conferences, a move away from the centralization characteristic after Trent. Along with the struggle to integrate many other liturgical changes, priests were now called to give special attention to the homily. How exactly did a "homily"—a word that had reentered the lexicon of the United States church after Vatican II—differ from a sermon? Was "sermon" a generic term and a "homily" something more specific? What did it mean to open up the treasures of the Bible more lavishly in a homily? Clarification was needed. Suddenly the homily assumed a greater importance in the liturgical life of the community.

Converging Forces

In the early 1970s, the National Conference of Catholic Bishops' Committee on Priestly Life and Ministry conducted a series of studies on the state of the American priesthood. These included *The Priest and Sacred Scripture*, a 1972 report of the Subcommittee on the Bible written by Eugene H. Maly and Barnabas Ahern, and *Spiritual Renewal of the American Priesthood*, a 1973 report of the Subcommittee on Spirituality written by Gerard T. Broccolo and Ernest E. Larkin. Msgr. Colin ("Scotty") MacDonald, executive director of the Bishops' Committee on Priestly Life and Ministry, had encouraged a highly collaborative approach to the generation of these and other documents and often served as facilitator for document development groups. His method was to identify and convene a team of experts from around the country with interest and expertise in the issues.

At the same time that the Bishops' Committee on Priestly Life and Ministry was focusing on the priesthood, other organizations were surveying the Catholic laity about issues related to the life of the church in the United States. These surveys, along with other research conducted in the 1970s, revealed a particular area of dissatisfaction within the Catholic community: the quality of preaching. A survey titled *The Mystery of Faith: A Study of the Structural Elements of the Order of Mass* (Washington, DC: United States Catholic Conference, 1981) was jointly conducted by the Federation of Diocesan Liturgical Commissions and the Bishops' Committee on the Liturgy; it polled Catholics asking their opinion of Catholic preaching. While only four of the 7,500 respondents said the homily ought to be dropped from the Mass, the majority noted that the quality of preaching was not very high. Criticism of Catholic preaching often focused on its lack of imagination, noting that, while the United States was a highly visual society, homilies tended to over-verbalize at the expense of imaginative metaphors and evocative images.

During this same time, scholarship began to focus on Catholic homiletics, and a number of studies and disserta-tions on Catholic preaching were published. John Burke's "The Development of the Theology of the Liturgical Sermon in the Formation of the Constitution on the Sacred Liturgy of the Sec-ond Vatican Council" (1968) described the homily as a distinct form. Willard Jabusch's sociological study of preaching, "An Exploration of the Crisis and New Approaches in Contemporary Catholic Preaching" (1968), offered insight into what listeners hear and highlighted the need for homilies that were more en-gaging, more conversational, and more accessible in wording and imagery. Leo R. Sands's "Contemporary Roman Catholic Preaching: Its Inventional Characteristics" (1975) examined 165 Catholic homilies in relation to the criteria of the Vatican II docu-ments and found little in their specific construction to represent the spirit or themes of these criteria. William Skudlarek's "Asser-tion without Knowledge: The Lay Preaching Controversy of the High Middle Ages" (1976) analyzed the history and charism of lay preaching. Skudlarek later participated in the development of *FIYH* and served as the principal writer of the document in its final form. Dialogue around preaching in the church was enlivened by these efforts.

Catholic seminaries responded to the call for improvement by expanding and enhancing the preaching curriculum. By 1981, a survey of forty-three Catholic seminaries in the coun-try revealed that preaching courses were specifically geared to liturgical preaching. These new courses focused on lectionary-based preaching, thereby differing in fundamental ways from the training that preceded the council, which had a more cate-chetical and moralistic emphasis. Now, only five out of forty-three seminaries offered a course other than liturgical preaching. The focus clearly was on preaching at the Sunday Eucharist.

The convergence of these forces precipitated an interest at the National Conference of Catholic Bishops (NCCB) in producing a contemporary document on homiletic preaching, with the goal of improving preaching throughout the Roman Catholic Church in the United States.

Fulfilled in Your Hearing *Is Commissioned*

In 1979, the Bishops' Committee on Priestly Life and Ministry commissioned the development of a document focused on pre-paring, drafting, and preaching an effective homily. This docu-ment would address key questions about the nature, function, and preparation of a homily, encourage both bishops and priests to respond to the need for ongoing development in the craft of homily preparation and delivery, offer practical information that would allow bishops and priests alike to improve the quality of their homilies, and provide the National Conference of Catholic Bishops with recommendations to improve homiletic preaching.

The subcommittee on Spiritual Renewal and Continuing Education of the NCCB's Committee on Priestly Life and Min-istry, chaired by Bishop William A. Hughes of Covington, Ken-tucky, was charged with this ambitious project. The development team was an ad hoc committee of twelve pastors and scholars specializing predominantly in the disciplines of Scripture, lit-urgy, and homiletics. The group, drawn from locations through-out the United States, included Bishop Thomas J. Murphy, S.T.D.; Richard J. Sklba, S.S.L., S.T.D.; William Skudlarek, O.S.B., Ph.D.; Thomas C. Brady, Ph.D.; Fred Baumer, C.PP.S., M.A.; Gerard T. Broccolo, S.T.D.; David Buttrick, B.D.; William Graham, M.A.; George T. Montague, S.M., S.T.D.; James Notebaart, M.A.; Robert Schwartz, S.T.L.; and Colin A. MacDonald.

Additional experts on the state of preaching and the needs of laity participated as consulters to the project at various points in its development. They included Rev. Andrew Greeley, Ph.D.; Rev. John A. Gurrieri, M.L., S.T.D.; Rev. Thomas Krosnicki, S.V.D., S.T.D.; and Mrs. Dolores R. Leckey, M.A. Unfortunately the minutes of these meetings cannot be found. Oral interviews with some members of this original committee, however, support the following narrative describing the development of *Fulfilled in Your Hearing*. The author conducted these interviews during the summer of 2008 with Fred Baumer, Gerard T. Broccolo, William Graham, Colin A. MacDonald, and William Skudlarek. Acknowledging that recollections can fade with time, the interviewees nevertheless provided an oral record of the events leading to the development and publication of this document.

The Committee's Work

The twelve members of the committee met seven times over the course of two years at a hotel near Chicago's O'Hare Airport, with sessions running from nine to five and participants flying in for the day. At the time, of course, no e-mail or conference calls facilitated the work in advance of the meeting, although an agenda was sent before each gathering. Sessions tended to be energizing and creative, with draft chapters being read, discussed, and revised. Msgr. McDonald, executive director of the Committee's Secretariat, was both experienced and accomplished in facilitating such groups. Participants remember him as someone who could draw out a wide range of ideas and who was adept at keeping discussion moving forward, even when opinions collided. After each meeting, typed notes were sent to participants for review and discussion at the next meeting.

Determining a Framework

As they began the process of drafting a document, the group was able to crystallize some "givens" with respect to preaching in a liturgical context. First, they unanimously recognized that preaching is integral to worship. Consistent with the teaching of the council and subsequent liturgical documents, preaching was not considered optional. The Sunday homily was not to be omitted without serious reason.

The group also recognized preaching as the primary duty of the priest, in agreement with the *Decree on the Life and Ministry of Priests*, issued in 1965 (4) and as noted in 1964 by Paul VI in his encyclical on the church, *Ecclesiam Suam* (90, 91). Paul VI's 1975 apostolic exhortation, *Evangelization in the Modern World*, also provided central organizing principles for the group, for example:

> The faithful assembled as a Paschal Church, celebrating the feast of the Lord present in their midst, expect much from this preaching, and will greatly benefit from it provided that it is simple, clear, direct, well-adapted, profoundly dependent on Gospel teaching and faithful to the magisterium, animated by a balanced apostolic ardor coming from its own characteristic nature, full of hope, fostering belief, and productive of peace and unity. Many parochial or other communities live and are held together thanks to the Sunday homily, when it possesses these qualities. (43; see also 42)

The committee also agreed that the mystery of Christ and the mystery of the church are "present tense" realities. God is still active, and the homily is a moment in which God's here-and-now activity is revealed. This was a central distinguishing factor for preaching within the Eucharist: because God is still at work among God's people, they are moved to praise and thanksgiving.

The group also concurred on the inherent creativity needed in homiletic preaching, approaching such preaching as fundamentally an act of offering a scriptural interpretation of life. And because there is more than one way to approach each text and more than one way to put texts in dialogue with each other, with the life of the community, and with events in the world, good preaching is never static or set. Although a particular understanding of a scriptural text may have been held in the past, changing times and differing circumstances of listeners, and especially current biblical scholarship, can cast the texts in a new light, and the preacher is called to respond and offer an interpretation of how God is acting here and now.

The creative dynamic within preaching calls for the recognition that each gathered assembly is a unique variable within the preaching moment. The group affirmed that preaching was always for a particular gathering of the baptized: preaching has to be for this people, at this time, in this moment. This realization would be expanded further and become a central guiding principle for *FIYH*.

Preaching Is within a Community

In the course of meeting over two years, the group grappled with the unique nature of homiletic preaching as a liturgical act. Recognizing that liturgical preaching takes place in a community of the baptized, the committee affirmed that liturgical preaching has some unique qualities that distinguish it from other kinds of preaching. For example, because the listeners are already believers, preaching at liturgy differs in fundamental ways from preaching as evangelization, in which the Gospel is preached to those who are not yet part of a worshiping community.

The committee concluded that preaching within ritual assumes that the listeners are a "we" and not an "I," a gathered community of believers, not simply isolated individuals with personal needs. Therefore, reflecting on who "we" are is central to the preacher's task. This is grounded in the highly incarnational theology that informs *FIYH*, which sees the living God still at work in the midst of the community.

The homily was perceived as an act of disclosing, in which God's presence in the lives and in the midst of the faithful is revealed. In the eucharistic liturgy, disclosing the signs of God's presence and activity is the major link between the word proclaimed and the turn to the table of the Eucharist. Recognition of God's work motivates the faithful to be grateful and to give praise—the liturgical connection that is unique to homiletic.

Mediating Meaning

Another key insight was the recognition that preaching should be part of *every* eucharistic and liturgical gathering. The Sunday homily alone cannot bear the entire burden of the preaching people need to hear, and other occasions and kinds of preaching need to be experienced, from daily preaching to days of recollection, retreats, and parish missions.

The group grappled with the distinction between catechetical preaching and the homily. Prior to the council, the emphasis in preaching was on catechesis, going back to the Council of Trent. Consistent with the vision of Paul VI's apostolic exhortation *Evangelization in the Modern World*, *FIYH* emphasized that explicating doctrines, expounding theological arguments, or exhorting people to live better lives were not the primary goals for a liturgical homily. Rather, as integral to the liturgical act in which believers participate, homiletic preaching leads first to recognizing God's active presence and then to responding to that presence in liturgy and a life lived in conformity with the Gospel.

Within the community of the faithful, then, the preacher functions as a "mediator of meaning," rather than a person focused on prescribing or proscribing behaviors. Looking at the human situation in the light of the Scriptures, the preacher discerns and expounds the intersection between the life of the community and the Gospel. *FIYH*'s homilist communicates from within the community, not above or beyond it. The homilist is a mediator of truth for this community: "The preacher does not so much attempt to explain the scriptures as to interpret the human situation through the scriptures" (20). Preaching is a pastoral process that changes particular lives; it is not a purely intellectual or academic undertaking.

Building on this understanding, the group judged that a quality homily had to begin not with the preacher, the text, or a particular methodology, but with an understanding of the gathered assembly. This insight was the natural byproduct of both the contemporary communication theory that had informed their thinking and the communion ecclesiology of Vatican II.

Placing the Assembly First

Using the assembly as the starting point led to a new approach to organizing the document itself. During early discussions, it was proposed that the document start with the preacher, moving then to consider the homily as an act of interpretation, and concluding with reflection on the assembly. Fred Baumer suggested, however, that the committee spend one working session focused on the distinction between communication as transmission (where a sender "delivers" or "sends" a message to a receiver) and communication as transaction (where a sender lives in a "world" of language, the receiver lives in a "world" of language, and meaning emerges when these two worlds fuse and understanding is born). A good homily creates tension by creating a world in language that may not exist outside that moment. It reveals a linguistic world of justice and peace that may not exist in a world outside of prayer but that, in this revelation, transforms listeners.

William Graham was also a strong proponent of approaching preaching as a communicative act with and for a specific group of people. As a professor of speech and drama and an experienced theater director, he continually reminded the group that successful ritual occurs when everyone within it is aligned in word and action. Drawing from his experience as a layperson in the pews, as well as his expertise as a professor of communication, Graham emphasized vitality and passion within preaching. The homily's success is dependent on the moment of utterance—the interface between the preacher, the listener, and a particular liturgical moment in which preacher/ritual/listeners come together. A homily is not something that lives on the page; it lives in the utterance, describing how God is acting now, and thus enabling the assembly to turn with praise and thanksgiving to the moment of the Eucharist.

William Skudlarek had been influenced by a preaching model that emphasized beginning with "the human." In this paradigm, preaching begins with a real, human situation and moves from that point of identification to the Scriptures, which in turn speak to the actual situation in the light of faith. Skudlarek suggested that homiletic is an act of interpreting the human situation from and through the Scriptures. Embracing this communications framework was another pivotal moment for the authors. Ultimately, the group arrived at the understanding of a homily as "a scriptural interpretation of human existence which enables a community to recognize God's active presence, to respond to that presence in faith through liturgical word and gesture, and beyond the liturgical assembly, through a life lived in conformity with the Gospel" (29).

No One Methodology

Although the group agreed on many points from the start, there were areas of contention. At the outset, some members thought the process of scriptural interpretation and its impact on a Catholic approach to preaching should be the starting point of the document. While this focus was included, it moved from the foreground as the conversation advanced.

Extensive discussion also revolved around the way to develop a homily. The preaching professors in the group locked horns on whether or not the document should recommend a particular approach to constructing a homily. Much attention was given to homiletician David Buttrick's approach of proceeding in "moves" that mirror the movement of the Scripture text. After two sessions of debate, the group decided that the preacher should not be pushed toward a single way of structuring the homily. *Fulfilled in Your Hearing* ultimately suggested a variety of strategies that could be incorporated in preparation while advocating a list of six "non-negotiables" considered essential to every preparation process.

The document also proposed a participative and inclusive approach to homily preparation. Taking the assembly as the starting point, the group recommended that preachers involve community members in their preparation. To this end, *FIYH* suggests a group preparation process with rotating membership and offers a seven-step format, providing discussion questions to structure meetings.

Naming the Document

The title *Fulfilled in Your Hearing* is taken from Luke's gospel. Jesus, after proclaiming several verses from Isaiah 61 to the community in the synagogue of Nazareth, declared that the fulfillment of the promise was occurring in that moment: "Today this scripture passage is fulfilled in your hearing" (4:21). The pericope described the dynamic that the group had articulated in their work, and a title was born.

Approving and Introducing Fulfilled in Your Hearing

Once the working sessions were complete, William Skudlarek was asked to serve as the writer for the group. Various individuals had produced chapter drafts, but Colin MacDonald wanted a single voice to shape the document's final draft. Gathering the input that had been generated, Skudlarek organized and synthesized the contributions, generating a draft with unity of style. After revisions by the committee, MacDonald presented the final draft to the members of the Committee on Priestly Life and Ministry for discussion and vote. The committee approved it unanimously.

Initially, bishops were responsible for distributing the document to the priests of their dioceses. According to USCCB Publishing, the first print run of 10,120 copies was made available in August 1982. There were eighteen printings through January 2005, with 94,341 units sold since first publication. The document is still in print, and, although it has been published only in English by the USCCB, unofficial French, Spanish, Polish, and Japanese translations also exist.

After *FIYH* was published, it was brought to the attention of the National Organization for Continuing Education of Roman Catholic Clergy (NOCERCC). Under the leadership of Gerry Thompson, NOCERCC developed and began offering workshops and retreats for bishops, clergy, and religious communities designed to transmit the principles of *FIYH* to the presbyterate in the United States. The most popular format for the workshop was a four-day retreat. It was presented in more than forty dioceses over the course of three years. Fred Baumer, John Galvin, Gerry Broccolo, and William Skudlarek developed and presented the workshop, which included four presentation areas, plus a preaching lab experience. The areas were described as follows: scriptural interpretation for preaching, the role of preaching in the liturgy, the preacher's spirituality and preaching, effective communication dynamics, and lab preaching with videotaping and feedback sessions.

The NOCERCC workshop was enthusiastically received. Suggestions about how to integrate preaching preparation with prayer practices helped priests find new avenues to authenticity and creativity in their preaching. Also, many priests had been trained to avoid revealing anything about themselves or their individual spirituality; now, appropriate self-disclosure was fostered and supported as an element that could profoundly animate preaching. Gerry Broccolo's contribution, both in the writing process and in the subsequent training sessions, was to redefine and emphasize the centrality of the preacher's spirituality in homily development.

Participants found the workshop helpful and instructive, and the response across the country was overwhelmingly positive. In participants' comments like "God was here," the facilitators saw the foundational concepts of *FIYH* affirmed. Connecting the document to a workshop proved key to building awareness and supporting the integration of its content in parish preaching.

The Response of Seminaries

In autumn 1984, fifty-seven professors of Catholic preaching met at the Catholic Theological Union in Chicago at the invitation of both CTU and the National Federation of Priests' Councils, then under the leadership of Rev. Richard P. Hynes, to discuss the role of *FIYH* in seminary education in preaching. At a subsequent meeting in 1985, the Catholic Association of Teachers of Homiletics was founded. By this time *FIYH* had become a standard text for homiletic preaching courses, appearing on almost every course syllabus. To the present day, it is a seminal text for preaching formation.

A Wider Audience

Fulfilled in Your Hearing also has been widely read beyond the presbyterate, particularly by those preparing for diaconal and lay ecclesial ministry in diocesan programs and seminaries. Aware that the preaching ministry might reach beyond the presbyterate, the committee decided that the major sections of the document would refer only to the "preacher," not the priest. This decision made its content accessible to a broader audience. In addition to forming preachers of the Word for over a quarter of a century, the insights offered by *FIYH* can be found in a growing literature in Roman Catholic homiletics.

Bibliography

Barbour, Claude-Marie. "Seeking Justice and Shalom in the City." *International Review of Mission* 73 (1984).

Benedict XVI. *The Sacrament of Charity.* Post-Synodal Apostolic Exhortation. Washington, DC: USCCB, 2007. Accessed at http://www.vatican.va/holy_father/benedict_xvi/apost_exhortations/documents/hf_ben-xvi_exh_20070222_sacramentum-caritatis_en.html.

Bergant, Dianne, with Richard N. Fragomeni. *Preaching the New Lectionary. Years A, B, C.* Collegeville: Liturgical Press, 1999–2001.

Bevans, Stephan. *Models of Contextual Theology.* 2nd ed. Maryknoll, NY: Orbis Books, 2002.

Bishops' Committee on Priestly Life and Ministry. *Fulfilled in Your Hearing: The Homily in the Sunday Assembly.* Washington, DC: USCCB, 1982. Accessed at: http://www.usccb.org/plm/fiyh.pdf.

Black, Cathy. *Culturally Conscious Worship.* St. Louis: Chalice Press, 2000.

Burghardt, Walter. *Preaching the Just Word.* New Haven: Yale University Press, 1996.

Craddock, Fred. *As One Without Authority.* Nashville: Abingdon, 1979.

D'Antonio, William V., James D. Davidson, Dean R. Hoge, and Mary L. Gautier. *American Catholics Today: New Realities of Their Faith and Their Church.* Lanham, MD: Rowman and Littlefield, 2007.

DeBona, Guerric. *Fulfilled in Our Hearing: History and Method in Christian Preaching.* New York: Paulist Press, 2005.

DeLeers, Steven. *Written Text Becomes Living Word: The Vision and Practice of Sunday Preaching.* Collegeville: Liturgical Press, 2004.

Doyle, Dennis. *Communion Ecclesiology: Vision and Versions.* Maryknoll, NY: Orbis Books, 2000.

Dysinger, Luke. "Accepting the Embrace of God: The Ancient Art of *Lectio Divina.*" Accessed at http://www.valyermo.com/ld-art.html.

Felder, Cain Hope, ed. *Stony the Road We Trod: African-American Biblical Interpretation*. Louisville: Augsburg Press, 1991.

Harris, Daniel E. *We Speak the Word of the Lord: A Practical Plan for More Effective Preaching*. Chicago: Acta Publications, 2001.

Heille, Gregory. *Theology of Preaching: Essays on Vision and Mission in the Pulpit*. London: Melisende, 2001.

Hilkert, Mary Catherine. *Naming Grace: Preaching and the Sacramental Imagination*. New York: Continuum, 1997.

John Paul II. *On Catechesis in Our Time*. Apostolic Exhortation. Oct. 16, 1979. Accessed at: http://www.vatican.va/holy_father/john_paul_ii/apost_exhortations/documents/hf_jp-ii_exh_16101979_catechesi-tradendae_en.html.

Krisak, Anthony F. "Theological Reflection: Unfolding the Mystery." In *Handbook of Spirituality for Ministers*, edited by Robert J. Wicks, 308–29. Vol. 1. Mahwah, NJ: Paulist Press, 1995.

Kysar, Robert, and Joseph M. Webb. *Preaching to Postmoderns: New Perspectives for Proclaiming the Message*. Peabody, MA: Hendrickson Publishers, 2006.

Lammers Gross, Nancy. *If You Cannot Preach Like Paul*. Grand Rapids: Eerdmans Publishers, 2002.

The Liturgy Documents: A Parish Resource, 385–414. Vol. 1. 4th ed. Chicago: Liturgy Training Publications, 2004.

Malina, Bruce M., and John J. Pilch. *Social-Science Commentary on the Letters of Paul*. Minneapolis: Fortress Press, 2006.

Malina, Bruce M., and Richard L. Rohrbaugh. *Social-Science Commentary on the Gospel of John*. Minneapolis: Fortress Press, 1998.

———. *Social-Science Commentary on the Synoptic Gospels*. 2nd ed. Minneapolis: Fortress Press, 2003.

New Interpreters Bible. 12 vols. Nashville: Abingdon, 1994–2002.

New Interpreters Bible Handbook of Preaching. Nashville: Abingdon Press, 2008.

Nieman, James R., and Thomas Rogers. *Preaching to Every Pew: Cross Cultural Strategies*. Minneapolis: Fortress, 2001.

Paul VI. *On Evangelization in the Modern World*. Apostolic Exhortation. Dec. 8, 1975. Accessed at http://www.vatican.va/holy_father/paul_vi/apost_exhortations/documents/hf_p-vi_exh_19751208_evangelii-nuntiandi_en.html.

Pazdan, Mary Margaret. "Biblical Criticism in the World of the Preacher." *Preach: Enlivening the Pastoral Art* (January/February 2006): 27–30.

Pennington, Basil. *Lectio Divina: Renewing the Ancient Practice of Praying the Scriptures.* New York: Crossroad, 1998.

Puskas, Charles B. *The Letters of Paul: An Introduction.* Collegeville: Liturgical Press, 1993.

Rahner, Karl. "Considerations on the Active Role of the Person in the Sacramental Event." In *Theological Investigations XIV: Ecclesiology, Questions in the Church, the Church in the World,* translated by David Bourke. New York: Seabury Press, 1976.

Schmitmeyer, Jim. *Preacher in a Hard Hat: A Guide to Preaching for Pastors and Everyone Else.* St. Louis: Chalice Press, 2006.

Schneiders, Sandra M. "Hermeneutics." In *The New Jerome Biblical Commentary.* Englewood Cliffs, NJ: Prentice-Hall, 1990.

————. *The Revelatory Text: Interpreting the New Testament as Sacred Scripture.* 2nd ed. Collegeville: Liturgical Press, 1999.

Skudlarek, William. "Spirituality and Preaching." In *Handbook of Spirituality for Ministers,* edited by Robert J. Wicks, 191–203. New York: Paulist Press, 1995.

Stone, Douglas, Bruce Patton, and Sheila Heen. *Difficult Conversations: How to Discuss What Matters Most.* New York: Penguin Books, 1999.

The Text This Week: Lectionary, Scripture Study, and Worship Links and Resources. Accessed at http://www.textweek.com/.

Tisdale, Leonora Tubbs. *Preaching as Local Theology and Folk Art.* Minneapolis: Fortress Press, 1996.

Untener, Ken. *Preaching Better: Practical Suggestions for Homilists.* New York: Paulist Press, 1999.

Van Harn, Roger, ed. *The Lectionary Commentary: Theological Exegesis for Sunday's Texts.* 3 vols. Grand Rapids: Eerdmans Publishers, 2001.

Wallace, James A. *Preaching to the Hungers of the Heart: The Homily on the Feasts and within the Rites.* Collegeville: Liturgical Press, 2002.

Waznak, Robert P. *An Introduction to the Homily.* New York: Paulist Press, 1998.

Webb, Joseph. *Preaching and the Challenge of Pluralism.* St. Louis: Chalice Press, 1998.

Wisdom, Andrew Carl. *Preaching to a Multigenerational Congregation.* Collegeville: Liturgical Press, 2004.

World Synod of Bishops. "Synod Message on the Word of God." *Origins* 38, no. 22 (Nov. 6, 2008): 341–49.